CATALOGUE OF THE MUSEUM OF ARCHAOLOGY AT SANCHI, BHOPAL STATE

Owing to the antiquity and rarity of this book, certain pages are regrettably absent, and readability is compromised due to the blurring of the original text. If you possess any insights regarding the availability of these missing sections, kindly inform us. Your assistance is crucial in ensuring the completion of this significant work for the benefit of future generations.

CATALOGUE OF THE MUSEUM OF ARCHAOLOGY AT SANCHI, BHOPAL STATE

MUHAMMAD HAMID

Published by

FacsiMile Publisher
12 Pragati Market
Ashok Vihar, Ph-2
Delhi - 110052, India
Phone: 011-47034999
Email: www.facsimilepublishers.com
info@facsimilepublishers.com

Distribution Network
gyanbooks.com
India, USA, Canada, UK, Australia

ISBN: 978-93-7106-017-2 (PB)
First Published, 1922

2nd Impression 2025

Printed at: Gyan Press, Delhi.

CATALOGUE OF THE MUSEUM OF ARCHAOLOGY AT SANCHI, BHOPAL STATE

Author: MUHAMMAD HAMID

Archaeological Survey of India

CATALOGUE

OF THE

Museum of Archaeology at Sanchi, Bhopal State

BY

MAULVI MUHAMMAD HAMID, B.A.,
(Excavation Assistant to the Director General of Archæology in India)

AND

PANDIT RAM CHANDRA KAK, B.A.,

AND

Mr. RAMAPRASAD CHANDA, B.A.,
(Archæological Scholars)

WITH A FOREWORD

BY

SIR JOHN MARSHALL, Kt., C.I.E., Litt.D., Ph.D., F.S.A.,
(Director General of Archæology in India)

CALCUTTA
SUPERINTENDENT GOVERNMENT PRINTING, INDIA
1922

FOREWORD.

This catalogue of antiquities in the Sanchi Museum has been designed partly as a complement to my already published *Guide to Sanchi* and partly as a supplement to the larger and more elaborate monograph on the monuments which is now in course of preparation. Neither the one nor the other of these books would have lent itself to a description of the many small and detached objects exhibited in the museum : the former, because the average visitor to Sanchi does not require detailed information about them ; the latter, because the inclusion of so much extra màterial would have made it unduly cumbersome.

The Museum at Sanchi has been built and furnished, and the exhibits arranged in it under my own personal supervision. The task of describing the exhibits has been delegated to three of my assistants, to Maulvi Muhammad Hamid, B.A., being assigned the stone sculptures, to Professor Ramaprasad Chanda, B.A., the inscriptions, and to Pandit Ram Chandra Kak, B.A., the iron and copper objects, the potteries and terracottas. Each of these scholars has received some measure of help from myself, and their descriptions have been examined and verified by my friend and collaborator, Mons. A. Foucher.

Of the antiquities now in the Museum some were found by me lying in the jungle which used to envelope the ruins, and others were unearthed during my excavations. With a few exceptions, however, such as the pottery from beneath the stone pavement round the Great Stupa, their find-spots offered little or no clue as to their date, for the reason that many of the objects had manifestly been transferred from older to later buildings and the débris of the ruined structures was too confused to admit of precise conclusions being drawn on the basis of its stratification. Hence the safest criterion to the age of most objects found on this site is their own individual style or technique ; and, so far as the sculptures are concerned, this criterion is not difficult of application. With the iron and copper objects and potteries the case is different, since sufficient materials are not yet available in India for that comparative study which is necessary in order to determine their chronological sequence. On the other hand, metal is less durable than stone, and it is unlikely that objects such as spears, knives, door-locks, hinges or the like were of any great age at the time when they were buried from view. Inasmuch, therefore, as nearly all of these iron objects were found in the débris of the Buildings 45, 46, etc., it may reasonably be presumed that they belong, with few exceptions, to the late mediæval epoch.

JOHN MARSHALL,
Director General of Archæology in India.

SIMLA,
July 24th, 1920.

SCULPTURES IN THE COURTYARD.

1. Statue (height 5′ 5″) of Buddha standing in the gift-bestowing attitude (*varadamudrā*) White grey sandstone. *Ūrṇā* and left arm missing; nose, lips and chin damaged. Hair in conventional ringlets. The upper garment (*saṅghāṭī*) covers both shoulders and arms and is spread out at the sides. It was caught up in the left hand, which was raised to the left shoulder. The border of the lower garment (*antarvāsika*) shows below the *saṅghāṭī* at the loins and above the ankles. The statue was broken across the neck and ankles. About 7th century A.D.

2. Statue (height 3′ 8″) of Buddha standing. White grey sandstone. Head, left shoulder, fore-arms and left half of the chest broken; feet detached but refixed; lower part of right leg damaged. Dress and attitude similar to No. 1. Inscription of two lines on the pedestal on either side of the feet contains the Buddhist creed in characters of about the 7th century A.D.

3. Image (height 2′ 4″) of Buddha standing. White grey sandstone. Head and fore-arms missing; drapery and toes of feet damaged. The style and attitude are similar to No. 1, but the right shoulder is bare. On the pedestal, to left, a kneeling female devotee with hands damaged; to right, similar male figure with a garland. About 7th century A.D.

4. Damaged torso (height 1′ 9″) of Buddha standing in the gift-bestowing attitude. White grey sandstone. Head missing; legs broken across thighs. Upper arm mutilated; left hand and thighs damaged. The *saṅghāṭī* covers both shoulders. About 7th century A.D.

5. Statue (height 3′ 6″) of Buddha standing. Pinkish grey sandstone. Head and fore-arms missing. The right hand was apparently held in the attitude of protection (*abhayamudrā*). The right shoulder is bare. The folds of the drapery hanging on the left are classical in character. About 7th century A.D.

6. Image (height 4′ 2½″) of Buddha standing on a damaged lotus. Dark purplish sandstone. Head, fore-arms and toe of left foot broken; right leg mutilated. Dress and attitude similar to those of No. 1. Behind the head is a damaged oval halo carved with lotus. On either side of the image stands a devotee holding *chaurī* and (?) stalk of lotus. About 7th century A.D.

7. Image (height 4′ 4″) of Buddha standing. Dark purplish sandstone. *Ushnīsha* and features damaged; left fore-arm and toes of right foot broken. Dress and attitude similar to No. 1. Lower garment (*antarvāsika*) shows above the ankles. On the left margin of the slab, inscription of one line containing the Buddhist creed. About 7th century A.D.

8. Image (height 3′ 5″) of Buddha standing on lotus. Buff-red sandstone. Head, right fore-arm and left hand missing. The dress and attitude are similar to those of No. 1, but the folds of the *saṅghāṭī* are still more stylised and the sculpture apparently belongs to a later period. On the pedestal, to right, is a female kneeling devotee; to left, a male. On the right margin of the slab is engraved an inscription of one line containing the Buddhist creed in characters of about the 7th century A.D.

9. Relief (height 5′ 1″) representing the subjugation of the mad elephant of Rājagṛiha. Buff-red sandstone. Head and left fore-arm of Buddha missing; chest, right arm, left leg

B

and feet damaged. Ornamental halo with garland-bearing gandharvas in clouds above. The right hand of the Buddha rests on the head of the elephant, behind which stands Indra holding *chaurī* in the right hand and *vajra* in left. The other attendant on the left, where we should expect Brahmā, resembles Buddha and holds a long staff in right hand. On the halo is an inscription of one line containing the Buddhist creed. Found near Stupa 6. About 7th century A.D. (Pl. I)

10. Fragment (height 2′ 1½″) of a relief of grey sandstone, illustrating the same scene. It contains the lower portion of the legs of standing Buddha with elephant bowing before him. To right of Buddha, remnants of an attendant standing behind the elephant, which is very well modelled. About 7th century A.D.

11. Fragmentary image (height 1′ 8″) of Buddha standing. Buff brown sandstone. Head, right arm, left fore-arm and legs below knees broken. Both shoulders wrapped in *saṅghāṭī*. The back-ground has disappeared. About 7th century A.D.

12. Image (height 2′ 2″) of Buddha standing. Brownish sandstone. Head, hands and feet missing. The *saṅghāṭī* covers both shoulders. A circular mortice (⅝″ diam.) near the right shoulder indicates that the right hand, which rested against the shoulder in the attitude of imparting security, was kept in position by means of a dowel. About 7th century A.D.

13. Damaged figure (height 2′) of Buddha standing. Brownish grey sandstone. Head, fore-arms and toes of feet missing. The *saṅghāṭī* covers both shoulders. The hands were evidently disposed in the *varadamudrā*. About 7th century A.D.

14. Headless statue (height 1′ 10″) of Buddha standing in the gift-bestowing attitude. Grey sandstone. Dress similar to No. 13. About 7th century A.D.

15. Torso (height 2′) of Buddha standing. Brownish sandstone. Head, feet and left hand missing; right hand damaged. Dress and attitude similar to No. 12. 7th-8th century A.D.

16. Statue (height including 2″ tenon at base, 2′ ½″) of Buddha standing on lotus in the gift-bestowing attitude. Dark purplish sandstone. Head and hands missing. Dress similar to No. 13. Defaced inscription of one line along the right margin of slab contains part of the Buddhist creed. Late Gupta.

17. Fragmentary image (height 2′ 2″) of Buddha standing. Reddish brown sandstone. Head, arms and legs below knees missing. Dress and attitude similar to No. 14. The statue was broken across the loins. 7th-8th century A.D.

18. Image (height 5′ 3½″) of Buddha standing in the gift-bestowing attitude. Dark purplish sandstone. Head and right fore-arm missing. Left fore-arm broken but refixed. The *saṅghāṭī* covers both shoulders and arms. It is spread out at sides and caught up in the left hand, which is held against the shoulder. Observe the prominent edges of the drapery on left. On the pedestal is a kneeling devotee to left. About 8th century A.D.

19. Statue (height 2′ 7½″) of Buddha of Mathurā stone seated cross-legged in the *dhyānamudrā*. Head detached but refixed: *ushṇīsha* broken; neck damaged; left earlobe, tip of nose and some fingers of the hands mutilated; and eyes and lips slightly injured. Hair treated in conventional ringlets. *Ūrṇā* mark on the forehead. Wears *saṅghāṭī* disposed in conventional folds and covering both shoulders and arms; the lower border of the *saṅghāṭī* shows on the throne beneath the legs of figure. On palms, wheel (*chakra*) symbol, and on soles of feet wheel and *triratna*. At the back of the head, mortice

about 1" square intended for a clamp. Possibly there was a nimbus behind the head. The sculpture was discovered from Stupa 14, where it was set up against the western wall of the relic chamber with a second wall built in front to protect it from damage. It is a product of the Mathurā school, but the features of the face, particularly the lips and eyes, and the highly conventionalised treatment of the hair and drapery proclaim it to be of the early Gupta age. The stupa in which the sculpture was found is assigned by Sir John Marshall to about the 7th century A.D. The image must therefore have been taken from a shrine of the early Gupta period when the latter had fallen to decay and enshrined there as an object of special veneration. This practice of burying older cult images in stupas was common during the mediæval period, as instances of it have also been found at Sārnāth, Sahēth Mahēth and other sites. (Pl. II)

20. Image (height 1′ 3″) of buff sandstone representing a figure of Buddha in sunk panel seated in meditation on a lotus throne. Head and thumb of left hand missing. *Saṅghāṭī*, in conventional folds, covering both shoulders and arms with its end falling on the seat. About 4th century A.D.

21. Image (height 1′ 6″) of Buddha seated in meditation on a throne supported by two lions. White grey sandstone. Head missing; left shoulder, hands and feet damaged. *Saṅghāṭī*, in conventional folds, covering both shoulders. 4th-5th century A.D.

22. Mutilated figure (height 1′ 11½″) of Buddha seated on a plain throne supported by two lions. Buff sandstone. The hands of the figure were probably disposed in the teaching attitude. Between the lions are two antelopes, crouching in the middle, face to face, with a wheel above their heads. Above the back of the lions and antelopes, two folds of hanging drapery. On the flat surface of the throne, on three sides of the image, inscription in characters of the Gupta period, reading :—

> *dēya........kha....ha chchha va Śrī-Kulādityasya yadatra puṇyaṁ tadbhavatu sarvvasatvānāṁ.*
>
> " (This is the pious) gift of Śrī-Kulāditya........let the merit of this (deed) accrue to all creatures."

23. Statue (height 2′ 10″) of Buddha seated cross-legged on a lotus throne supported by two lions. Buff sandstone. Head detached but refixed. Right arm and shoulder and part of chest broken; left earlobe, fingers of left hand and big toe of right foot damaged; features slightly injured. Hair and *ushṇīsha* treated in schematic ringlets. The right shoulder is bare and the lower end of *saṅghāṭī* shows on the lotus seat. The left hand is placed in the lap holding end of *saṅghāṭī* in palm; the right was probably held in the *abhayamudrā*. Lotus symbol on the sole of right foot. On pedestal, a male and a female kneeling devotee between the lions: the male, who wears a pointed beard, in the attitude of adoration, the female carrying a garland. 6th-7th century A.D. (Pl. III)

24. Statue (height 3′ 3″) of Buddha seated in meditation on a lotus throne supported by two lions. Buff sandstone. Face chipped off; left knee broken; chest and right arm damaged. *Saṅghāṭī* thrown over both shoulders and its end spread on the throne. Circular nimbus with lotus and bead decoration, flanked by two garland-bearing gandharvas in clouds. Wheel symbol on soles of feet. The devotees on the pedestal are treated in the same way as in No. 23. On either side of Buddha, about the level of the shoulders

B 2

is an inscription of 3 lines containing the Buddhist creed in characters of the 6th-7th century A.D.

25. Statue (2′ 3½″) of Buddha seated in the teaching attitude on a lotus throne supported by two lions. Buff sandstone. Head, right arm and left fore-arm missing; right half of chest mutilated; and toes of feet damaged. Dress similar to No. 23. Behind the shoulders, remnants of a halo. On pedestal, between the lions, two kneeling devotees—one in adoration, the other carrying a garland. 6th-7th century A.D.

These three sculptures (Nos. 23-25) have a close resemblance to each other and may have been carved by one and the same sculptor.

26. Pedestal and crossed legs of a Buddha figure of buff red sandstone seated on inverted lotus supported by two lions (height 2′ 4″). The left hand, in lap, holds end of *saṅghāṭī* in the palm; the right, of which the fingers only remain on the right knee, was disposed in the earth-touching attitude (*bhūmisparśamudrā*). An end of *saṅghāṭī* is spread on the throne. Apart from the wheel, which also appears on the palm of the left hand, the soles of feet bear a number of other symbols, *viz.*, a shield, a pair of fish, a staff with flag, a goose or shell, an elephant goad, a trident, an umbrella and a *swastika*. The symbols on the left foot have disappeared, but the wheel is distinctly visible. The space between the lions is occupied by an elaborately embroidered cloth hanging from the throne. The petals of the lotus bear a portion of the Buddhist creed. Below the lion on proper left is a Sanskrit inscription in Nāgarī characters of the 9th or 10th century A.D. It consists of a stanza in the Sragdharā metre of which two *padas* are legible and read as follows :—

L. 1. *Om Prā....āyushy* ....
[*Ta*] *syākhyāyāḥ kilantē Sugataguṇa vṛitaḥ saṁsthito bhadra*................
L. 2. *savdaḥ* [*I*]
o vā o .... *sam*
sam........*dēdharmoyam k* [*ri*] *tasya pravarasukhakarajñānasaṁ*
L. 3. .... *prāptayē saḥ* [*II*]

" Verily his name stood selected in the end by virtues of the noble path..........This is the proper gift of..........for the attainment of knowledge which brings about the mighty happiness of the Krita age."[1]

27. Statue (height 3′ 8″) of a Bodhisattva standing against a pilaster. Grey sandstone. Head detached but refixed; face damaged; right hand and foot and left arm and leg broken off. Wears ornamental headdress, necklaces, armlets, girdle with hangings and a long garland. Slightly oval halo decorated with lotus. The left hand rested against the thigh, the right probably held stalk of lotus (?) 8th-9th century A.D.

28. Statue (height 2′ 2″) of Bodhisattva seated cross-legged on a double lotus throne. Dark purplish sandstone. Head, right arm and left fore-arm missing; toes of feet damaged. Wears ornaments. The hands were apparently disposed in the preaching attitude. 9th-10th century A.D.

29. Statue (height 3′ 7⅜″) in the round, of a Bodhisattva figure (Vajrasattva ?) seated crosslegged on a lotus throne supported by two lions and by stems of a lotus plant springing from the pedestal. Purplish sandstone. Head and arms missing; legs damaged. Wears

[1] Bühler, Ep. Ind., II, p. 370.

necklaces, pearl-garland and anklets. Remnants of long curls of hair falling on shoulders and of an elaborate halo behind. The right hand apparently holds a mutilated thunder-bolt (*vajra*) in front of the breast; the left, probably a bell on hip. On the pedestal, to proper right, remnants of a kneeling devotee; to left, a miniature replica of the principal image. Above, on either side of the lotus throne traces of attendants, the right foot of the attendant on the right resting on a *bhadraghatta*. About 10th century A.D.

30. Torso of a Yaksha (height 2′) of brownish sandstone with arms upraised perhaps to support a throne. Wears *dhoti* with band tied in front and necklace with three ornaments, two of which are in the shape of *nandipadas*. Early School.

31. Torso (height 2′ 1″) of a Yaksha similar to No. 30. These figures are in the round. Also compare the capitals of the western gateway of Stupa I.

32. Statue in the round (height 2′ 7″) of a corpulent male figure of brownish sandstone, probably Jambhala, seated in the easy posture on a four-legged chair. Left leg hanging down. Head, arms and right leg below the knee broken off; chair damaged. Wears necklace and girdle. On the chair, on either side of the image, ends of scarf(?). About 4th century A.D.

33. Pedestal and legs of a female deity (Tārā ?) seated in the easy posture on a lotus springing from the pedestal (height 1′ 6″). Buff sandstone. Right leg partially damaged. Wears ornamental girdle and anklets. The right foot rests on a lotus stool. On the pedestal, to proper right, figure of a nude, pot-bellied *preta* squatting with hands upraised to receive the nectar which is flowing from the fingers of the deity; to left, a female figure seated on a cushion with an axe (*paraśu*) in her right hand and lotus in the left. Between this figure and the right foot of the diety, three kneeling devotees on a lotus carry garlands. Above the central image, some human figures in vertical compartments to left and an ornamental cushion to right. About 9th century A.D.

34. Damaged sculpture (height 1′ 1″) of grey sandstone similar to No. 33. On the pedestal, two female attendants, one on either side of the deity, apparently hold lotus stalks in their hands. The attendant on the left is four-armed. In front of the pedestal, mutilated figures of a kneeling devotee to left and a pot-bellied *preta* to right. About 9th century A.D.

35. Image (height 2′ 4″) of a six-armed goddess (Tārā ?) standing on a cushion and wearing ornaments. Grey sandstone of Udayagiri. Head, extra left arms, normal right fore-arm and all hands, excepting one on the right, broken; breasts damaged. In the only hand that has survived destruction, the goddess holds the handle of a sword. On either side of the deity, two female attendants stand one behind the other; the figures in the front row hold *chaurīs*, those in the back, lotuses. On either side of the cushion of the goddess, remnants of two kneeling devotees. 9th-10th century A.D.

36. Image (height 4′) of a 4-armed goddess (Chunda?) seated cross-legged on a lotus throne. Grey sandstone of Udayagiri. Face and breasts chipped off; hands and knees damaged. Wears ornaments. The upper hands are raised to the shoulder: the left apparently holding a lotus, the right a lotus and a rosary. The lower right hand is disposed in the charity *mudrā*, the left holds an uncertain object in the lap. Above the mutilated halo is a Buddha figure, in meditation, with a goddess on his left seated in the *līlāsana* and holding lotus in the left hand. Traces of two devotees on the pedestal. 10th-11th century A.D.

37. Fragmentary sculpture (height 1′ 6″) of greyish sandstone representing the waist and legs of Durgā killing the buffalo demon (*mahishāsura*). The goddess wears a beaded girdle, anklets and sacred thread. Her right foot is placed on the demon's breast which is being pierced with a trident. The back of the buffalo is so doubled that the haunches nearly touch the head. About 12th century A.D.

38. Image (height 1′ 9″) of a goddess seated in the easy posture (*līlāsana*) on a lotus springing from the pedestal. Purplish sandstone. Head and right forearm missing; left hand, knees and feet damaged. The goddess wears ornaments and holds a full-blown lotus (*padma*) in her left hand. On either side of the deity are two female attendants standing one above the other and holding *chaurīs*. The upper figure on the right is almost entirely lost. Below the left knee of the goddess and looking up to her is a female devotee seated on the pedestal in the attitude of prayer. About 10th century A.D.

39. Image (height 2′ 3¾″) of a god, perhaps *Mayūravidyārāja*, seated in the easy posture on a double lotus throne which is supported by his *vāhana*, the peacock. Head missing, and right hand and foot damaged. Wears elaborate necklace with curious pendants, armlets, girdle and anklets. The right hand rests against the knee with palm turned outward; the left holds stalk of blue lotus (*utpala*), springing from the pedestal below. About 10th century A.D.

40. Statue (height 3′ 8″) of a standing *chaurī*-bearer of grey sandstone. Head missing; chest and hands damaged. Wears ornaments and shoulder-belt which passes over the left shoulder and under the right armpit. Plain nimbus behind the head. The left hand held a *chaurī* of which the handle is broken; the right rests against the thigh. Traces of a stalk of lotus (?) encircling the right arm. The back slab is curved at the top. The figure probably served as the right hand attendant in a large group. About 10th century A.D.

41. Fragmentary sculpture (height 1′ 11″) of reddish grey sandstone representing the waist and legs of a male figure standing between round pilasters. Left foot detached but refixed; toes of right foot and part of left leg below the knee broken; hands slightly damaged. Wears ornaments, sacred thread and a long garland which shows in front of the knees. The left hand of the figure rests against the thigh, the right holds the handle of a sword on hip. On the pedestal, fore-part of a curious animal to left. Late Mediæval.

42. Sculpture (height 2′ 9″) of grey sandstone representing Kuvera, standing between round pilasters and wearing ornaments. The right hand apparently holds a blue lotus against the shoulder; the left is stretched down and holds a money-bag. Near the right foot of the deity, bust of a *yaksha* figure. Probably used in the face decoration of a structure. About 8th century A.D

43. Sculpture (height 3′ 1″) of grey sandstone representing Varuṇa standing between round pilasters. Wearing elaborate head-dress, ornaments, garland and sacred thread. The right hand holds an uncertain object before the breast; the left is stretched down and holds a noose (*pāsa*). Near the left foot is the fore-part of a *makara*. Late Mediæval.

44. Section of a door-jamb of purplish grey sandstone carved on three sides and gradually stepped in from sides to front. The carving on the sides consists of a pot and foliage design surmounted by undulating scroll work. On front, figure of a deity standing in a pillared niche, holding uncertain object (flower ?) before the breast. Curious object near the right foot. About 10th century A.D.

45. Section of a pilaster (height 4′ 6½″) of grey sandstone with an offset 6½″ wide in front. Plain upto 2′ 4″, with the exception of a spear-mark on the central offset. The carving is divided into three bands by an *āmalaka* pattern below and a diamond design above. The lowest band contains foliated designs and figurines inside half or quarter circles. In the middle band are Buddha, Bodhisattva or attendant figures in rectangular niches, the attendants carrying *pūrṇa kumbhas*. In the upmost band are *kīrtimukha* heads spouting forth *Kinnaris* with single serpent-hoods and double snake-tails and with their hands held in the attitude of prayer. The spear mark on the lower portion was apparently added at a later period. At the back is a mortice about 6½″ square. Late Mediæval. (Pl. IV)

46. Door-jamb (height 2′ 5″) of grey sandstone. The carving on the front is divided into two facets. The left facet contains, from below, a male figure standing in a pillared niche, lotus and scroll decoration, vase and foliage design and remnants of scroll work. The pillared niche in the other facet contains a female figure standing with a *padma* in her left hand. Above thenicle is a leogriff standing with one of his hind legs on the back of an elephant, the other resting on the chest and left hand of the *mahāut* who is sitting with doubled legs on the head of the elephant with his head turned towards the tail of the animal. The fore-legs of the leogriff are dangling in the air and a *yaksha* is hovering above him. Observe the flowing tail and horns and the curious collar-shaped mane of the leogriff. Late Mediæval.

47. Door-jamb (height 3′ 1½″) of reddish brown sandstone. Front divided into four facets. The facet to extreme left is plain; the one next to it represents a pilaster of the pot and foliage type decorated with *kīrtimukha* heads and foliated designs; the other two facets are adorned with floral decorations. About 7th century A.D.

Pavement slabs, pillars, cross-bars, etc., bearing Prakrit inscriptions in archaic Brāhmī characters.

48. Semi-circular fragment (15″ by 8¼″) of a pavement slab of brownish sandstone bearing the following inscription :—

Viṇhumitasa dā [*naṁ*]
"The gift of Viṇhumita (Vishṇumitra)."

49. Fragment (15¾″×14″) of a pavement slab of grey sandstone bearing the following inscription :—

........*m* [*ā*] *tu Bhādāsiriya dānaṁ*
"The gift of Bhādāsiri (Bhadhrāśrī), mother of ....
......................."

50. Fragment (15″ × 11¼″) of a pavement slab of reddish grey sandstone with a fragmentary inscription of one line reading :—

........*putasa bhichhuno d* [*ā*]
"The gift of the monk........son of ...."

51. Fragment (13¾″×12½″) of a pavement slab of brownish grey sandstone bearing the following inscription :—

Nēhanipad [*a*] [*va*]................,

52. Fragment ($12\frac{1}{4}'' \times 11\frac{1}{2}''$) of an inscribed slab of buff red sandstone. The inscription reads :—

................*takasa bhātu*............

53. Fragment ($9\frac{1}{4}'' \times 6\frac{1}{2}''$) of a pavement slab of purplish sandstone with the remnants of an inscription of 2 lines reading :—

L. 1. ....*y*....
L. 2. [*ma*] *tasa Arahadi*

54. Fragment ($13\frac{3}{4}'' \times 11''$) of a pavement slab of brownish grey sandstone from the site of Monastery 19 bearing the following inscription :—

........*sa bh* [*i*] *chhuno dānaṁ*.
"The gift of the monk................"

55. Broken slab ($2'\ 1'' \times 1'\ 7\frac{1}{2}''$) of brownish sandstone from Stupa I, bearing the following inscription :—

Vedisikāya bhikhuniya Ga............
"The gift of the nun Ga......of Vedisa."

56. Similar broken slab ($1'\ 8\frac{3}{4}'' \times 1'\ \frac{1}{2}''$) from Temple 40 bearing the following inscription :—

Ājimuditāye—"(The gift) of Ājimuditā."

57. Similar fragmentary slab ($1'\ 8'' \times 1'$) from Temple 40 with the following inscription :—

Kurarāya Sirikāya.........
"(The gift) of Sirikā (Śrīkā) of Kurara."

58. Inscribed fragment ($1'\ 3\frac{3}{4}'' \times 1'\ 2\frac{3}{4}''$) of purplish sandstone. The inscription reads :—

Dhamakasa........

59. Fragment ($1'\ 1\frac{1}{4}'' \times 10\frac{1}{4}''$) of a pavement slab of brownish grey sandstone from Stupa I bearing an inscription of 2 lines :—

L. 1................*riyā Mitasiriyā*
L. 2..................*dā* [*naṁ*]
"The gift of......Mitasiri (Mitraśrī)."

60. Inscribed fragment ($1'\ 7\frac{1}{4}'' \times 8\frac{1}{4}''$) of a pavement slab of buff grey sandstone with spots of an amethyst colour. Found at the site of Temple 40. The inscription reads as follows :—

...........*Nāgarikā*
"(The gift of) the citizens..........."

61. Fragment (Ht. $1'\ 6\frac{1}{2}''$; width $\times 9''$) of an octagonal pillar of grey sandstone bearing an inscription of one line on front reading :—

upāsikāya Himarakhitāya dānaṁ
"The gift of the female lay worshipper Himarakhitā."

Found in debris to the S. W of Stupa I.

62. Inscribed fragment ($12\frac{1}{4}'' \times 7\frac{1}{2}''$) of an octagonal pillar of grey sandstone from Temple 40 :—

............*dāna* [*tha*] *bho*

" This pillar is the gift of..........."

63. Fragment (height 9") of a similar pillar from Temple 40 bearing......*Sihara*.... in Brāhmī characters :—

64. Fragment (height $1' 4\frac{1}{4}'' \times 1' 9''$ thickness) of a similar pillar from Temple 40. Remnants of an inscription of 2 lines on face :—

L. 1.............*Mārasavasa*

L. 2.............*datasa dānaṁ*

"...............

65. Fragment (height 1′ 9″) of a similar pillar of buff grey sandstone with 2 lines of Brāhmī inscription reading :—

L. 1. Kaṁṭakañ [*ūya*] *kā* [*naṁ u*] *pā*

L. 2. sakānaṁ dānaṁ

" The gift of the lay worshippers of Kaṁṭakañu."

66. Fragment (height 1′ 9″; side of square 9″) of a pillar of purplish sandstone from Temple 40. Square below and octagonal above. Brāhmī inscription of 2 lines in front on the square portion reads :—

L. 1. Avoda Barāyasikha

L. 2. [*sa*] *dānaṁ goṭiyaṁ du tha*

L. 3. bho.

" (These) two pillars are the gift of the guild of Barāyasikha of Avoda (Arbuda)."

67. Fragment (height $1' 6\frac{1}{2}''$) of a similar pillar from Temple 40 bearing the following Brāhmī letters :—

L. 1. U [*je*] *niyā*

L. 2. dāna

68. Fragment (height 1′) of a similar pillar from Temple 40. Brāhmī inscription of 2 lines in front on the square section reads :—

L. 1. Tākāripadā

L. 2. Samikasa dānaṁ

" The gift of Samika (Svāmika) of Tākāripada. (Tākārapada ?)."

69. Fragment (height $11\frac{1}{2}''$; width 1′ 2″) of a similar inscribed pillar of brownish grey sandstone from Temple 40. Inscription in Brāhmī :—

L. 1. ....*dha ṅa m*..........

L. 2. ....[*ku*] *lasa dānaṁ.*

70. Broken cross-bar (length $2' \frac{1}{2}''$; ht. $11\frac{1}{4}''$) of brownish grey sandstone from the ground railing of Stupa III bearing the following inscription in later Brāhmī characters :—

Dhamagirisa bhikhuno Pērikupasa dānaṁ

" The gift of the monk Dhamagiri (Dharmagiri), inhabitant of Perikupa."

71. Broken cross-bar (1′ 11½″; height 1′ 3½″) similar to No. 70. Inscription reads :—

Dhaṁmadāsasa dānaṁ

"The gift of Dhammadāsa."

Pillars and Umbrellas of the Early School.

72. A square pillar (height 3′ 11″; thickness 5¼″) of dark-grey sandstone probably serving as newel post in a solid balustrade. On the inner face, now turned to front, is a vertical groove about 1½″ broad and 1″ deep, running along the whole length of the pillar. Traces of tenon at the top. About 2nd century B.C.

73. Lower portion of a pillar (height including 6″ tenon at base 3′ 8″; width 11½″; thickness 8″) of buff-red sandstone probably belonging to Temple 40. It is rectangular below and octagonal above. The alternate sides of the octagon are 4″ and 4½″ in width and the smaller sides are fluted. The peculiar chamfering of the edges where the square shaft is changed into octagon is characteristic of the Early School. About 2nd century B.C.

74. Lower portion of a pillar (height 4′ 1″; width 9¼″; thickness 8¾″) of dark grey sandstone probably belonging to Temple 40. Square below and octagonal above. The alternate sides of the octagon are 5″ and 3″. The pillar is rough dressed upto 1′ 3½″. About 2nd century B. C.

75. Section of a pillar of buff brown sandstone. (height 3′ 7¼″; thickness 9″). Square below and octagonal above. The sides of the octagon measure 3″ and 4½″ alternately. Observe the peculiar chamfering of arris at the point of transition where the shaft is changed into octagon. About 2nd century B.C.

76. Section of a sixteen sided pillar of grey Udayagiri sandstone. Height 4′ 8¾″. The lower portion is rectangular (10″ × 8¾″) and rough dressed upto 2′ 10″. The sixteen sided section is 8¾″ in diameter, the sides varying from 1½″ to 2″ in width. About 1st century B.C.

77. Section (height 5′ ½″ × 8¼″) of an octagonal pillar of buff-red sandstone, bearing a Brāhmī inscription of one line about the middle. The inscription is engraved on two sides and reads :—

Datakalavāḍasa dānaṁ

"The gift of Datakalavāḍa." 1st-2nd century B.C.

78. Umbrella (diam. 2′ 9¼″; thickness 4″) of dark purplish sandstone provided with a square hole (4¾″ each way) in the centre for the tenon of the staff. Parts of the rim and underside have chipped off. Perhaps from Stupa 4.

79-80. Two fragments (11″ × 8½″ × 3½″ thick and 9½″ × 8¾″) of an umbrella of reddish-brown sandstone decorated with radiating ribs on the underside. Found on the terrace of, and probably belonging to, Stupa 2.

Berm Railing of Stupa II.

81. Section of a pillar in 2 pieces (height 2′ 6″; width 7½″) decorated on the front with a half lotus at the top and a lion in the central medallion.

82. Lower half of a pillar (height 1′ 2¾″ × 7¼″). Half lotus in the lower and remnants of a complete one in the central medallion.

83. Lower half of a pillar (height 1′ 7¼″; width 8″). Half lotus below and legs of a bull in the central medallion above.

84. Lower half of a pillar (height 1′ 8½″). Half lotus below and *nandipada* shaped ornament alternating with lotus leaves above.

85-87. Lower halves of 3 pillars (heights 1′ 8¼″; 1′ 6½″; and 1′ 4½″) ornamented in the same way as No. 82.

88. Lower half of a pillar (height 1′ 6″). The space between the lower and the central lotus is occupied with a floral design.

89. Middle portion of a pillar (height 1′ 8″). The central lotus is surrounded by a wreath of flowers.

90. Upper half of a pillar (height 11′ 9″) decorated with lotuses at back and bearing the following Prakrit inscription in archaic Brāhmī characters on the front :—

L. 1. Nadinagarā
L. 2. Asadavaya bhikhuya dāna

"The gift of the nun Asadeva (Aśvadevī) from Nadinagara (Nandinagara)."[1]

91. Upper half (height 1′ 5½″) of a similar pillar. The inscription consists of one line in archaic Brāhmī characters and reads :—

Patiṭhānasa

"The gift of Patiṭhāna (Pratishṭhāna)."

92. Upper half (height 1′ 8¼″) of a similar pillar. The inscription reads :—

Chiratiya bhichhuniya dānaṁ.

"The gift of the nun Chiratī."[2]

93. Fragment (height 1′ 8½″) of a pillar. Conventional palmette in the central medallion. Observe the peculiar turn of the leaves.

94. Fragment (height 9½″; width 9″; thickness 6¾″) of a railing pillar. The central medallion is relieved with a palm tree standing in an enclosure of the balustrade pattern. These two pillars apparently belong to Stupa I.

95. Fragment (height 1′ 3½″) of a corner pillar from the stairway railing of Stupa II. Carved on 3 faces. *Front face.*—Waist and legs of a male figure standing in the upper panel, and head and uplifted arms of a figure in the lower. *Left face.*—Lower halves of a male and a female figure in the upper panel, and upper halves of a similar couple, wearing tunics and pointed caps, in the lower. *Right face.*—Legs of a male and a female figure standing in the upper panel, and busts of a couple in amorous attitude in the lower

96. Fragment (height 1′; width 3¾″; thickness 2¾″) from the middle section of a pillar. *Yaksha* with uplifted arms above and a floral design surrounded by a *nandipada* shaped ornament below.

97. Fragment of a pillar (height 1′ 3½″) with a half lotus in the top medallion.

98. Fragment (height 1′ 3½″) of a pillar with a fragmentary lotus in the central medallion.

99. Fragment (height 8¼″; width 7⅞″; thickness 3¼″) of a pillar containing a plant with mango shaped berries in the central medallion.

[1] Bühler, E. I., II, p. 400, No. 53: Luders' List No. 629.
[2] Bühler, E. I., II, p. 399, No. 48; Luders' List, No. 624.

100. Fragment (height 1′ ¼″) of a pillar. In the central medallion is a curious animal with human face and bull's body and horns. (Pl. XI)

101. Fragment (height 11¼″; width 7¾″; thickness 4½″) of a pillar, decorated with a mounted horse set on a lotus flower in the central medallion.

102. Top portion of a pillar (height 9¾″). The half medallion is decorated with a curious winged animal resembling a deer.

103. Top portion of a pillar (height 10″×7⅛″). Half lotus at back. Brāhmī inscription of two lines on front reads :—

L. 1. Budharakhitaya Bhichhuni [*ya*]

L. 2. dana

"The gift of the nun Budharakhita (Buddharakshitā.)"[1]

104. Top portion of a pillar (height 10½″). Half lotus at back. Brāhmī inscription of one line on front, reading :—

Is [*i*] *dataya Bhikhuniya dana.*

"The gift of the nun Isidata (Ṛishidattā)."[2]

105. Fragment (height 7¼″) of a corner pillar decorated on three sides with floral designs and fruit trees.

106-108. Fragments of 3 pillars (heights 9½″; 9¾″; and 8½″) relieved with half lotuses in the lower medallions.

109. Lower portion (height 7½″) of a pillar. Half medallion relieved with a pair of *Sāras* birds standing with a young one in the middle.

110. Fragment of a pillar (height 9½″) with remnants of a palmette design in the central medallion.

111. Fragment of a pillar (height 8¼″). Vase and foliage design in the central medallion.

112. Fragment of a pillar (height 9½″) with remnants of a palmette design in the central medallion. This design is different from that on No. 110.

113. Fragment of a pillar (height 5¼″) from the stairway railing, bearing remnants of half lotus below and a Brāhmī inscription of one line above reading :— ....*jadatasa dāṇaṁ*

114. Top portion (height 10½″) of a pillar. Half lotus at back and Brāhmī inscription of three lines on front. The inscription reads :—

L. 1. [*Na*] *kulasa bhi* [*chhu*] *no dānaṁ*

L. 2. ayasa Nakhatanāmasa

L. 3. atevāsino

"Gift of the monk Nakula, the pupil of the Reverend Nakhata (Nakshatra)."

115. A similar fragment (height 10½″) with a Brāhmī inscription of 2 lines reading :—

L. 1. ....bhikhuniya

L. 2. [*Ku*]*rarāya*

116. Similar fragment (height 7½″) with inscription of one line reading :—

Asaetaya (?) *Bhavadevaya d*[*ā*]*nam*

"The gift of Bhavadeva of Asaeto (?)."

[1] Bühler, E. I., II, p. 401, No. 61; Luders' List No. 637.
[2] Bühler, E. I., II, p. 399, No. 44; Luders' List No. 620.

117. Fragment in two pieces (length 2′ 4″; height 8¾″; thickness 9″) of a coping stone from the harmikā railing of Stupa 2. On face, undulating lotus design badly damaged.

Fragments from the balustrades of other Early Stupas.

118. Lower half (height 1′ 8½″) of a pillar from the stairway railing of a stupa. The decoration consists of a half lotus below and a complete one in the central medallion.

119. Corner pillar (height 2′ 3½″; width 8″; thickness 6½″) from the stairway railing of a stupa carved on two faces with half lotuses at the top and bottom and a full lotus in the middle.

120. Section of a small railing pillar (height 1′ ¾″; width 5¼″; thickness 4¾″) with lotuses in the lower and central medallions.

121. Fragment (height 1′ 2½″; width 6¼″; thickness 5½″) of railing pillar decorated in the same way as No. 120.

122. Fragment (height 1′ 4″; width 6¼″; thickness 5½″) of a small railing pillar bearing a half lotus in the lower medallion. The lower portion of the pillar is rough dressed upto a height of about 8″, indicating that the baluster belonged to the harmikā railing of a stupa.

123. Fragment (length 1′ 4″; height 11⅝″; thickness 10½″) of a coping stone of greyish buff sandstone decorated with undulating lotus design on the face. Probably from the harmikā railing of Stupa 4.

124. Fragment (length 1′ 2½″; height 11⅛″) of a coping stone of buff coloured sandstone from the harmikā railing of a stupa with undulating lotus design on front. About 1st-2nd century B.C.

125. Section of a coping stone (length 2′ 11½″; height 11″ × 9″) from the harmikā railing of a stupa. Buff grey sandstone. The face is relieved with full blown lotuses alternating with a debased honey-suckle or palmette pattern—a design more appropriate for the decoration of a vertical upright than for a horizontal coping stone. The projecting rim above the decoration has disappeared.

126. Fragment (length 1′ 3⅜″; height 8″; width 7″) of a coping stone from the berm railing of a stupa bearing a Brāhmī inscription of one line at the top, reading :—

Rāño Su [haḍa] datasa Kosagharikasa........

"(The gift) of King Su [haḍa] data (Subhatadatta) of Koshagṛiha."

127. Similar inscribed fragment of a coping stone (length 1′ 1″; height 8¾″; width 7½″). The inscription reads :—

Vāsiṭhiputasa Kusumakasa dānaṁ

"The gift of Kusumaka, son of Vāsiṭhi (Vāsishṭhi)."

This and the preceding fragment were brought from Kāchhī Kānakheṛa, a village some 3 miles south-west of Sāñchī.

128. End piece (length 2′ 1¼″; height 9¼″; width 8½″) of a coping of grey sandstone from the harmikā railing of a stupa, relieved with an undulating lotus design on the face.

129. End piece (length 1′ 11″) of a coping stone possibly from the same harmikā railing as No. 128.

130. Fragment (height 2′; width 1′ 1″; thickness 5″) of buff-grey sandstone from a late *torana* with volutes on the projecting end and two small mortices on the false capitals probably for pegs for hanging garlands on.

Architectural pieces—Gupta and Late Mediæval.

131. Top portion (height including 2″ tenon 2′; thickness 10¼″) of an octagonal Persepolitan pillar of buff-grey sandstone. Bell-shaped capital adorned with overturned lotus leaves on the shoulder. Above, cable necking surmounted by a plain circular abacus. Gupta imitation of Śuṅga.

132. Top portion (height 1′ 7½″; including tenon 1′ 10½″; thickness 9½″) of a Persepolitan pillar of grey sandstone. Circular shaft, reeded bell-shaped capital surmounted by a cable necking and square abacus. Early Gupta.

133. Fragment (height 9½″; width 11½″) of a pilaster of pinkish grey sandstone. At the top is a wreath and lotus design which originally ornamented the base of a vase capital. Between this and the sixteen sided shaft below is the leaf and half-disc decoration fully described in No. 136 below. Late Gupta.

134. Top portion (height 1′ 4½″; width 1′ 2½″) of a pilaster of dark purplish sandstone consisting of a vase and foliage capital surmounted by a square abacus. Late Gupta.

135. Pillar (height 4′ 8½″) of buff-grey sandstone with streaks of a purplish colour on the lower portion. Rough and square up to 2′ 4½″. The round tapering shaft above is surmounted by a bell-shaped capital, cable-necking and a small square abacus. Late Gupta.

136. Section of a pillar of brownish-grey sandstone. (height 3′ 9½″; thickness 8¼″). Square upto 2′ 4″, and changed into octagonal and sixteen sided above. The sides of the octagon and hexadecagon are alternately fluted and flat, and each is surmounted by a half disc, the angular spaces between the discs being occupied with leaves. Above the half discs in the sixteen sided section, the shaft becomes circular and the half disc decoration is repeated—the discs however being inverted. Above this are the remnants of a wreath and lotus design which ornamented the base of a vase capital. Late Gupta.

137. Upper portion of a pillar of brownish-grey sandstone. height 2′ 7½″; thickness 8½″. The shaft is octagonal below and sixteen sided above, with the sides alternately fluted and flat. A sixteen sided vase serves as capital. It is decorated at the base with a row of lotus petals surmounted by cable ornament, the former being also shown at the top as coming out of the mouth of the vase. The pillar is then changed from the circular into octagon and thence into square—the square portion serving as the abacus. Late Gupta. (Pl. IV)

138. Upper portion (height 2′ 7¾″×9″) of a pillar of dark purplish sandstone with streaks of a grey colour. Octagonal below and sixteen sided above. The square abacus and the vase capital below are treated in the same way as in the previous pillar. The decoration of the portion below the vase is exactly similar to that of the corresponding portion in No. 136. Remnants of a circular mortice at the top. Late Gupta.

139. Fragment (height 1′ 6½″; diam. 9½″) of a pillar of dark purplish sandstone, octagonal below and sixteen sided above. Similar to No. 138.

140. Fragment (height 2′ 3⅞″) of a plaster af dark purplish sandstone with a square base. The shaft is square below and octagonal above, the square portion releived with a vase and foliage design. Late Gupta.

141. Fragment (height 2′ 1″, width 1′ 3¼″) of a door-jamb of grey sandstone. The carving on the front is divided into two facets. The facet on the right contains, from below, an arched roof of a shrine, a *Kīrtimukha* head, vase and foliage pattern and a scroll

ornament. In the other facet are remnants of a lion standing upon an elephant behind the roof of a shrine. About 7th century A.D.

142. Fragment (height 2′ 1$\frac{3}{4}$″ ; width 6$\frac{3}{4}$″) of a pilaster of buff-grey sandstone. In the lower portion, head of a *yaksha* in front and the fore-part of an elephant surmounted by a standing leogriff behind. To right of the figures is a square pilaster in relief; and above the pilaster a four-armed figure of Śiva seated in the easy posture and holding trident, vase and cobra in his hands. Below the right knee of Śiva is the bull Nandi. About 7th century A.D.

143. Fragment (height 1′ 11″ ; width 1′ 1$\frac{1}{2}$″) of a door-jamb of grey sandstone. The carving on the front is divided into two facets by a round pilaster in the middle. To right of the pilaster is a female figure standing, with a water-pot in front of breast; to left, a *yaksha* supporting the fore-part of an elephant, on the head of which appear the hind legs of a leogriff. 7th-8th century A.D.

144. End piece of a frieze stone of dark purplish colour. Length 1′ 4$\frac{1}{2}$″ ; height 11″. Decorated on the front and right hand face with *Kīrtimukhas* spouting forth bells and pearl-garlands, the ends of the latter being caught in the mouths of leogriffs set back to back one on either side of the *Kīrtimukhas*. About 8th century A.D.

145. End piece (length 1′ 6$\frac{1}{4}$″ ; height 11$\frac{1}{4}$″) of a frieze stone resembling No. 141 in all respects.

146. Section of a heavy (?) pilaster of brownish grey sandstone. Height 3′ 5″ ; width 1′ 7$\frac{1}{4}$″ ; thickness 1′ $\frac{3}{4}$″. Carved on three sides and carving divided into two bands of ornament by an *āmalaka* and lotus pattern. The lower band contains an elaborate vase and foliage design ; the upper scroll work is surmounted by a band of leaf ornament. 8th-9th century A.D.

147. Damaged capital (height 2′ 5$\frac{1}{2}$″ × 1′ 5$\frac{1}{4}$″) of a pilaster of the pot and foliage type. Dark purplish sandstone. Above the vase is a raised band of scroll work. Towards the top of the fragment, are the legs of a flying *gandharva* flanked by two *nāgas* with five headed serpent-hoods and terminating below the waist in curled serpent tails. Small tenon at the top. About 8th-9th century A.D.

148. Fragment (height 1′ 11$\frac{1}{2}$″ × 1′ 9$\frac{1}{2}$″) of a door-jamb of dark purplish sandstone. Carving on front divided into two facets. In the left hand facet, head and arms of a *yaksha* below and mutilated figure of Buddha above; in the right hand one, similar *yaksha* below and a standing male figure wearing *dhoti*, elaborate head-dress and ornaments above. About 9th century A.D.

149. Fragment (height 1′ 7$\frac{1}{4}$″ ; width 1′ 4$\frac{1}{2}$″) of a (?) door-jamb of dark purplish sandstone divided into two facets. Male figure standing in a pillared niche in the right hand facet; female in the left. The figures wear elaborate dress and ornaments and hold *padmas* in their uplifted left hands. They may perhaps represent the *Padmapāṇi* with an attendant goddess. About 9th century A.D.

150. Fragment (height 1′ 9$\frac{1}{2}$″ × 8″) of a stele of buff-red sandstone. Female figure seated cross-legged on a lotus throne below; traces of another female standing on a lotus above. About 9th century A.D.

151. Damaged sculpture (height 1′ 7$\frac{1}{2}$″ × 1′ 3″) of dark purplish sandstone. In a pillared niche in front is a mutilated figure of Buddha seated in the earth-touching attitude. 8th-9th century A.D.

152. Pillar (height 4′ 11½″; thickness 1′ 6½″) of buff-grey sandstone. Cruciform (twenty sided) in shape. Plain upto 2′ 3¾″. The upper portion is adorned with four bands of ornament separated from each other by strings of beads. These bands contain from below—tridents with leaf shaped central prongs, *kīrtimukha* heads, vase and foliage designs, and in the uppermost band, a row of large leaves with foliage falling on either side of each leaf. Late Mediæval.

153. Pillar (height 4′ 9¼″; thickness 1′ 5½″) of buff-grey sandstsone, similar to the preceding one, but with only the three upper bands of ornament and a diamond mark below, the *Kīrtimukha* head in front. The carved bands are separated from each other by a cable ornament below and a lotus design above. Late Mediæval.

154. Door lintel (length 4′ 9″; width 1′ 10¾″; height 9½″) of reddish grey sandstone. The front face is recessed in the middle and flanked on either side by a flower-vase in high relief placed between square pilasters. The sides and the recessed portion on front, are decorated with a row of ornamental pendants below, and of diamond designs above. The pendants bear a close resemblance to upturned vases. 9th-10th century A.D.

155. Door lintel (length 2′ 11½″; width 1′ 2½″; height 7½″) of dark-grey sandstone. The face is adorned with a plant design in the centre and two *kīrtimukhas* at the sides. A pair of geese is perched amongst the branches in the central design. 9th-10th century A.D.

156. Upper portion of the back slab of a Buddhist image of dark purplish sandstone. Height 2′ 6″; width 2′ 5″. Remnants of halo decorated with lotus petals, about the middle; and traces of the figure of a Dhyāni Buddha above. On either side of the Dhyāni Buddha, Sanskrit inscription of two lines in acute-angled characters of about the 8th century A.D. It contains the Buddhist creed and reads as follows :—

L. 1. ye dhammā[1] *hetu-prabhavā hetuṁ teshāṁ tathāgato hyavadatu*[2] *teshāṁ cha*

L. 2. yo nirodha evamvādī mahāśramaṇaḥ (11)

"Of all objects which proceed from a cause the Tathāgata has explained the cause, and he has explained their cessation also; this is the doctrine of the great Śramaṇa."

Architectural stones from Temple 45.

157. Face stone (length 2′ 5½″; width 1′ 6½″; height 11¼″) from the *śikhara* of Temple 45. Buff-grey sandstone. Face decorated with niches and foliage. Late Mediæval.

158. Carved stone (length 3′ 1″; ht. 1′ 7″) from a niche in the *śikhara* of Temple 45. The carving on the front consists of the upper portion of a large niche flanked by a garland-bearing *gandharva* on either side. Above this is a conventional floral design with lion's head spouting forth a bell resting on the apex of the niche below. About 7th cent. A.D.

159. Face stone (length 1′ 3″; ht. 1′ 7″) from the *śikhara* of Temple 45 decorated with niches, foliage and geometrical designs ranged in three rows one above the other. Grey sandstone. Late Mediæval.

---

[1] Read *arma.*
[2] Read *avadat-teshāṁ.*

160. Capital (length 2′ 3″; ht. 8½″) of a pillar of grey sandstone. Cruciuorm in shape (twenty sided). The sides are slightly raised, spread out and relieved with ribs resembling the ribs of the *āmalaka* fruit. The capital is placed upside down. Late Mediæval.

161. Face stone (length 1′ 11½″; width 1′ 8″; ht. 1′) fr om the *śikhara* of Temple 45. Decorated with niches and floral designs. Buff-grey sands tone. Late Mediæval.

162. Face stone (length 2′ 2″; ht. 1′ ¼″) from the *śikhara* of Temple 45. The front and the right hand face are ornamented with arched roof of a shrine thrice repeated and relieved with niches and foliated patterns. Grey sandstone. Late Mediæval.

163. Face stone (length 2′ 1¼″; ht. 1′ 8½″) from the *śikhara* of Temple 45. The carving on front resembles the arched roof of a shrine surmounted by a trident-shaped finial. A circular niche in the centre contains the head of a lion, below which is a double dentil ornament. Buff grey sandstone. Late Mediæval.

164. Carved stone (length 2′ 10½″; ht. 11½″) from the *śikhara* of Temple 45. The front and left hand face are relieved with niches and half niches. Buff grey sandstone. Late Mediæval.

165. Carved stone (length 2′ 6″; ht. 5¼″) from the *śikhara* of Temple 45. Front and right hand face relieved with raised ribs like those of the *āmalaka* fruit. Grey sandstone. Late Mediæval.

166. Face stone (length 2′ 1½″; ht. 1′ 7″) of a purplish grey colour from the *śikhara* of Temple 45, relieved with arched roof of a shrine on front. Late Mediæval.

167. Face stone (length 3′ 5″; ht. 1′ 3½″) from the *śikhara* of Temple 45. Arched roof of a shrine on front, flanked by two miniature shrines each with a diamond design in the interior; between the roof and the side shrines are recessed spaces, also occupied by diamond patterns. Grey sandstone. Late Mediæval. (Pl. IV)

168. Face stone (length 3′ 2″; ht. 10½″) from the *śikhara* of Temple 45. Decorated with niches in the same way as No. 164. Late Mediæval.

169. Face stone (length 2′ 3½″; ht. 1′ 7½″) from the *śikhara* of Temple 45. Decorated with arched roof of a shrine on front. Late Mediæval.

Votive Stupas.

170. Votive stupa (height 3′ 1″) of dark-purplish sandstone with a square base. Around the middle of the drum is an ornamental frieze with *kīrtimukhas* spouting forth pearl garlands. Below the frieze is a small niche on the front face containing a seated figure of Buddha in the *bhūmisparśa-madrā*. The stupa bears three short inscriptions in Nāgarī characters of 8th to 12th century A.D., one above the frieze, the other two on the square base. A square mortice at the top shows that the missing *hti* and umbrella were carved out of a separate block. Late Mediæval.

171. Votive stupa (height 2′ 8¼″) of dark purplish sandstone. Umbrella missing. Octagonal base adorned with eight niches each containing a figure of Buddha standing in the *abhaya* or *varada* attitude. Above the dome is the harmikā or *hti* with a square mortice at the top for the umbrella staff. Late Mediæval.

172. Votive stupa (height 2′ 5½″) of grey sandstone. *Hti* damaged and umbrella missing. On front, Buddha seated in meditation in a niche. Late Mediæval.

D

173. Votive stupa (height 2′ 9½″) of grey sandstone. Umbrella missing. Late Mediæval.

174. Votive stupa (height 2′ 5½″) of grey sandstone. *Hti* and umbrella missing. Around the base are four niches each containing a seated figure of Buddha. Late Mediæval.

A.—Sculptures in the Roofed Hall.

A1. Capital (height 6′ 10½″; width across the abacus 3′) of Aśōka Column consisting of a bell-shaped cap with cable necking and a circular abacus surmounted by the fore-parts of four lions set back to back, the whole finely finished and polished to a remarkable lustre from top to bottom. Buff sandstone of Chunār.

The bell has been pieced together from a number of fragments and partially restored in plaster of Paris. It is decorated with sixteen conventional petals in the Persepolitan style. The abacus, a part of which has also been restored, is ornamented with four honey-suckle designs separated one from the other by beautifully sculptured geese in pairs confronting each other with lowered heads.

The capital was broken across the cable necking. The lions crowning the abacus "though sadly disfigured still afford a noble example of the sculptor's art. Mark in particular the spirited vitality of the animals........the tense development of their muscles, the swelling veins, the strong set of claws and the crisp treatment of the mane disposed in short schematic curls."[1] The depressions in the eye-balls of the geese and lions show that precious stones were probably inserted in these places and apparently affixed to the stone with shellac or some similar material as no pins appear to have been used. (Pl. V)

A1. (a) Fragment (Ht. 11″, width 5″) of a petal from the bell of No. A1.

(b) Another fragment (6″×3″) from the bell of No. A1.

(c) Another fragment (3½″×2½″) from the bell of No. A1.

(d) Fragment (Ht. 9½″) from the abacus of No. A1. The decoration consists of the back half of a goose and part of a honey-suckle flower.

These four fragments were discovered in debris some time after the restoration of the capital.

A2. Broken umbrella (length 1′ 11½″; width 1′ 1½″; thickness 7½″) of highly polished buff Chunār sandstone pieced together from several fragments and partially restored. Outer side plain; under-side relieved by four concentric bands, about 2¾″ apart, with radiating ribs between. The ribbed side is convex but changes into concave near the fourth band. The ribs between the third and the fourth concentric bands are separated from each other by shorter ribs, about 1¼″ long, emanating from the fourth band towards the centre. Traces of similar radiating ribs beyond the fourth band. Found in the debris of Stupa I. Probably belonged to the original brick stupa of Aśōka's time. (Pl. VII)

A3. Fragment (1½′×7½″×2¾″) in four pieces of an umbrella of highly polished buff sandstone of Chunār. Delicately carved ribs on the underside. Mauryan.

A4—A6. Three fragments (9⅜″×5½″; 10⅝″×5¼″; 5″×4″) of an umbrella of buff sandstone of Chunār. Similar in all respects to the one described above. No. A5 is in two pieces. Mauryan.

A7. Fragment (2¾″×1½″ by 1⅛″ thick) from the outer rim of a similar umbrella. Underside relieved with radiating ribs, the outer ends of which are covered by a fine undulating fillet. The edge of the rim is also marked with shallow grooves. Mauryan.

These fragments (A3—A8) were found from the debris of the Great Stupa. The material

[1] Sir John Marshall, *Guide to Sanchi*, p. 91.

Chunār sandstone) of which they are made and the exquisite precision with which they are chiselled, combined with the brilliancy of their polish leave little doubt that they were manufactured during the Maurya age and in all likelihood belonged to the original brick stupa of Aśōka's time. Numbers A4—A7 are not adorned with any concentric bands such as are to be seen on A3.

A8. Fragment (length 10½"; width 6"; thickness 5¾") of an umbrella of buff sandstone of Chunār. Inner side convex and relieved by concentric bands with radiating ribs between. The polish of the stone has disappeared. Probably Mauryan.

A9. Fragment (length 8"; width 6¾"; thickness 3¾") of an umbrella similar to the preceding one. The carving on these two fragments is not half so delicate as that on Nos. A3—A8. Probably Mauryan.

A10. Standard bowl (height 2' 5¼") of Mauryan workmanship, of highly polished buff Chunār sandstone, pieced together from fragments and partially restored. It consists of a square moulded base, octagonal tapering shaft with fluted sides, surmounted by a cup-shaped capital —also eight-sided—on which rested the bowl. The sides of the bowl are missing. The restoration of the base is not quite certain; it may have been somewhat larger or smaller. (Pl. VI)

A10(*a*). Fragment (height 10") of an octagonal pillar. Tapering shaft with fluted sides. Two of the sides are broadened towards the lower end which was probably provided with a tenon. Highly polished buff sandstone of Chunār. Mauryan.

A11. Fore-part of an elephant (length 2' 6"; height 1' 11½") of greyish sandstone. Trunk and legs missing; left eye damaged. Observe the modelling of the animal's head and the folds on the neck. The sculpture was found from debris in Temple 40 and was broken and in its present condition before the columns bearing early Brāhmī inscriptions were erected. About 2nd-3rd century B.C.

Fragments from the gateways of Stupa 1.

With the exceptions of the pillars which are rough dressed at back, these fragments are all carved in the round. They are also of white grey sandstone except a few which come from the South Gateway where a slightly purplish stone has been used.

A12. Fragment (height 2' 3½"; width 2'; thickness 1' 7½") from the western pillar of the South Gateway. The carving on the front face has peeled off. The right or inner face bears the legs of a door-keeper standing armed with a broad Indian sword and wearing a close-fitting tunic, (?) shirt and boots. Near the feet, remnants of a lion to left, and an uncertain object to right. The pillar is broken across the ankles of the door-keeper. The left or outer face is decorated with an undulating plant design containing creepers, mangoes and other fruit trees with jewelled necklaces hanging from their branches and birds perched amidst the foliage, eating berries. In the lower left corner is the bust of a grotesque *yaksha* wearing the same sort of necklace as Nos. 30 and 31, and holding the springing of the scroll work in his hand.

A13. Fragment (height 1' 1½"; width 1' 11"; thickness 10") of the same pillar as A12. The relief on the front face contains a headless female figure descending from a couch or chair to left and mutilated legs and tail of a horse to right. The lady wears a transparent *dhoti* and a scarf. At the back of the chair is an uncertain object; and behind the horse what might be the legs of a standing human figure. The inner face has peeled off; but a pearl necklace and remnants of a creeper still exist on the left or outer face.

A14. Fragment (height 1′ 10″; width 1′ 9″; thickness 1′ 1″) of the same pillar as A12 and A13. The carving on the front and inner faces has disappeared. The outer face, now turned to front, bears the figure of a monkey and a pearl-and-stone necklace above and remnants of a flowing floral design below.

A15. Section, in eight pieces, of the east jamb of the South Gateway. Ht. 8′ 7″; width 1′ 11″; depth 1′ 9½″. The top of the pillar is missing and the lower portion is broken off across the eyes of the door-keeper on the inner face.

Almost all the scenes represented on this pillar relate to the incidents immediately before or after the *Sambodhi* or enlightenment of the Buddha. (Pl. VIII)

Front face.—The lower panels on the front face have totally disappeared; the remaining three panels at the top are more or less mutilated.

Top panel. Episode of the Nāgarāja Muchalinda.—After attaining enlightenment the Buddha fasted for 49 days and spent the period, successively, under the Bodhi, the Banyan, the Muchalinda and the Rājāyatana trees. While seated under the Muchalinda tree the Buddha was shielded from rain by the hood and coils of the Nāga king Muchalinda. Here, towards the top of the panel, we see the trunk and lower branches of the Muchalinda tree decorated with garlands and flanked by a flying garland-bearing *kinnara* on either side. In front of the tree is the throne of the Buddha, and in the fore-ground, the Nāgarāja seated on rocks or his own serpent coils. On either side of the Nāga king are two queens seated on wicker stools, and behind them are female attendants holding *chauris*. The Rāja has a five headed serpent-hood; the females have only one hood each.

Second panel. Offering of the bowls by the four Lokapālas.—The story is that on the last day of his long fast of 49 days after the enlightenment, when Buddha was seated under the Rājāyatana tree, two merchants, Tapussa and Bhalluka, made an offering to him of barley-cakes and honey. The Buddha having no bowl in which to receive the offerings, four bowls of stone were brought by the guardians of the four quarters (*Lokapālas*) and Tathāgata commanding them to become one took the food and ate it. In the relief we see Buddha, represented by his throne, seated under the Rājāyatana tree, which is surmounted by an umbrella and flanked by a *kinnara* on either side carrying garlands and offerings. To the left of the tree are two *Lokapālas* carrying bowls with two attendants, one of which is apparently a *gandharva* playing on a harp. To right, is the bust of another *Lokapāla* holding a bowl in his hands. The other figures on the right have disappeared.

Third panel.—Bullock cart drawn by a pair of oxen in the centre surrounded by horsemen and attendants, one of the latter walking in front of the bulls and carrying a spouted vessel. There are only three figures in the bullock cart but sufficient remains to show that originally there were four of these—the missing figure being probably that of the driver. Behind the cart is a dog licking its right foot. The scene apparently represents a caravan moving towards the left and probably refers to the visit of the two merchants Tapussa and Bhalluka who made an offering of barley-cakes and honey to the Buddha on the last day of his long fast of 7 weeks. This scene should, according to the texts, have preceded the scene of the offering of four bowls. (Pl. VIII)

Left or Inner face. *Top panel.*—In the centre of the panel is a throne placed in front of a tree on either side of which is a celestial riding on *suparna* and carrying offerings.

Below the celestials are five male devotees standing to left and four to right with a female devotee stooping on either side of the throne. To the right of the throne is the entrance to the enclosure in which the tree is situated. The meaning of the scene is not clear.

Second panel.—In the centre of the relief is the throne of Buddha placed in a pavilion carried on octagonal pillars and flanked by garland-bearing *gandharvas.* The cupola of the pavilion is relieved with niches and surrounded by a balustrade. Above the throne is a curious circular object badly mutilated. Two male devotees stand to right, and a male and a female to left of the throne. The scene has not been identified.

Third panel. Approach to the Bodhi seat.—The diamond throne of the Budhha is placed under a garlanded *pīpal* tree flanked by flying *kinnaras* carrying garlands and open baskets containing offerings. A male and a female devotee stand on either side below. Of the couple on the right, the female is carrying a casket: while the male, who is no other than Svastika the grass cutter, is stooping and cutting grass with a scythe. In the corresponding figures on the left the male (who is presumably a *deva*) is carrying the bundle of grass cut by Svastika and the female is standing in devotional attitude.

Fourth panel. Offering of the milk-rice to the Buddha by Sujātā.—In the centre of the panel, Buddha represented by his throne, sitting under the *Nyagrodha* tree which is surmounted by a garlanded umbrella and flanked by garland-bearing *kinnaras*. To the left of the throne is Sujātā bringing the milk-rice to Buddha. She is attended by a female servant who is stooping by the side of the throne while her spouted water-vessel is placed on the ground. The male figure in the left lower corner of the panel is presumably a *deva* watching the pious action of the virtuous Sujātā. The figures are repeated on the right.

Fifth panel.—Towards the top of the panel is the promenade (*chaṅkrama*) of Buddha decorated with garlands. In front of the promenade, four female figures probably representing the daughters of Māra trying to seduce the Buddha. In the group to left, we see them turned into old hags and in the right hand one, after they have been restored to youth again,

Lowest panel.—The upper portion of the door-keeper's head is all that remains in this panel.

Back.—The back is plain except that the top portion is carved with a large lotus flower and traces of a railing and a standing figure remain in a niched panel above.

Outer face.—The outer face was ornamented with full blown lotus flowers enclosed by an undulating lotus design on either side. (Pl. VIII)

A16. Fragment in two pieces (height 2′ 7″; width 2′ 1″; thickness 1′ 1¾″) from the bottom portion of the pillar described above. The carving on the front face has almost entirely disappeared. The outer face, now turned towards the front, bears the head of a *makara* below and lotus flowers above.

A17. Fragment (height 12¼″; width 1½′; thickness 4″) of the same pillar as A16. On front, lower portion of a relief containing the mutilated throne of Buddha above and a water-pond with lotuses and ducks below. On either side of the throne, remnants of attendants. Traces of a flowing floral design on the right or outer face.

A18. Fragment in five pieces (Ht. 1′ 9½″) of the same pillar as A16. Undulating lotus design on the outer face. On front, remnants of two sculptured panels. In the lower panel, male figure seated on a chair with two females, one holding an umbrella over his head, the other entertaining him with her dancing; in the upper panel, legs of a female figure.

A19. Fragment (height 1′ 7″; width 1′ 1½″; thickness 10½″) from the north pillar of the West Gateway. On the outer face, now turned to front, is the head of a griffin facing left with remnants of the vine creeper above.

A20. Fragment (height 2′ 11½″; width 1′ 11″; thickness 2′ 4″) in two pieces from the same pillar as A19. The carving on the front has peeled off. The inner face, now turned to front, bears the mutilated figure of a door-keeper wearing the usual dress and ornaments and standing under a flowery tree. The pillar is broken off below the knees of the door-keeper.

A21. Fragment (height 1′ 2½″; width 2′ ½″; thickness 6½″) of a pillar from the South or West Gateway. On front, remnants of two sculptured panels. Parasol decorated with garlands and flanked by devotees in the lower panel and legs of elephant in the upper. On the right hand side, throne placed in front of a tree with a spouted vessel to its right.

A22. Fragment in four pieces of the western end of the lowest architrave from the South Gateway (Length 3′ 6½″; ht. 1′ 11″; height including griffin 3′ 7½″; thickness 1′ 3″). On front, volutes to left and portion of tree with the head of a peacock facing a scorpion to right. On the back, to right volutes; to left, a boy advancing towards a crouched antelope and legs of another human figure behind the boy. Remnants of the wings of a flying *gandharva* on the outer end. The volutes were only fragmentary and have been completed on both sides in plaster of Paris.

The griffin at the top was found detached but most probably belongs to the South Gateway. It is broken across the neck and feet and sadly disfigured. Observe the beak, the hair on the throat, the curious scaly mane along the neck and the band of indented ornament round the mouth.

A22(*a*). Small fragment (length 1′ ¼″) belonging to A22. Carved with foliage and right foot and tail of a peacock.

A23. Fragment in five pieces of the eastern false capital and lateral projection from the middle architrave of the South Gateway. Length 7′ 1″; height 1′ 11¼″; height including griffin 3′ 7½″.

Front.—The false capital is relieved with a pair of horses one behind the other. The architrave ends in a volute. Between the volutes and the false capital, elephant in a lotus pond. Above the elephant, a seated female figure; to her left, legs of another figure, who apparently played on the harp, one end of which rests on the lady's legs; to right of the lady, a casket suspended on a bracket and below the bracket what might be a water vessel.

Back.—On the false capital, a pair of bulls, one behind the other. Between the bulls and the volutes, an elephant with a young amidst trees.

The griffin at the top was broken in two pieces and is exactly similar to the one described in A22.

A24. Branch of a mango tree (Ht. including 6¼″ tenon, 2′ 6″; width 1′ 7½″) from one of the larger brackets supporting the lowest architrave of South Gateway. Foliage on the outer side, with a parrot perched in the upper branches. The carving on the other faces has disappeared.

A25—A26. Damaged torse of a large *yakshi* standing under a tree.

A25. The tree (height including $4\frac{1}{2}''$ tenon, $2' 1''$; width $2' 6''$) bears elongated leaves and bunches of fruits. (Pl. IX)

A26. The *yakshi* (height $2' 9\frac{1}{4}''$) wears two long chains which pass over the shoulders and hang as far down as the hips, crossing each other below the breasts and at the back. The transparent under-garment is tied by a plain band and a beaded girdle. The hair is arranged in two thick plaits the ends of which are joined. Three jewelled garlands forming part of the head-dress hang on the back. The figure does not belong to the same bracket as the tree under which it stands; the *yakshi* comes from the south end of the East Gateway, the tree probably from the South Gateway. The *yakshi* was broken across the loins. (Pl. IX)

A27. Branch of a mango tree (Ht. $3' \frac{1}{2}''$; width $2' 9''$) in three pieces with the left arm of a *yakshi* in front. The fore-arm of the *yakshi* is decorated with bangles and jewelled wristlets and a branch of the tree is held in the hand. Probably from the West Gateway.

A28. Mutilated torso of a large *yakshi* (height including $5\frac{3}{4}''$ tenon, $3' 3\frac{1}{2}''$; width $2' 11\frac{1}{2}''$) standing under a mango tree. The right forearm rests on a branch of the tree. The treatment and ornamentation of the hair and undergarment are exactly similar to No. A26. Probably from the West Gateway. (Pl. IX)

A29. Fragment (height $1' 2\frac{1}{4}''$; width $1' \frac{1}{2}''$) of a large tree with left foot of a *yakshi* figure.

A30. Fragment (height $1' \frac{1}{2}''$; length $1' 10\frac{3}{4}''$) of a large tree with feet of *yakshi*, probably forming part of No. A25.

A31. Mutilated left hip (height $1' \frac{3}{4}''$) of a large *yakshi*. Remnants of *dhoti* at back and of a beaded girdle above the hip.

A32. Fragment (height $11''$) of the leg of a large *yakshi* wearing anklets.

A33. Mutilated arm (Ht. $1' \frac{1}{4}''$) of a large *yakshi* wearing bangles, with remnants of tree behind. The tree is similar to A25 and the fragment appears to have formed part of the same.

A34. Fragment (height $7\frac{3}{4}''$) of a flowery tree with elongated leaves probably from the same bracket as A25 and A33.

A35. Damaged elephant (height $1' 3\frac{3}{4}''$) with remnants of rider and servant probably from the East Gateway (lowest architrave, south end). End of trunk missing; head, eyes, ears and tusks damaged. The elephant is covered with two striped *uttar chhadas* one above the other. A part of the lower *uttar chhada* is thrown back over the legs of the rider and in its falling folds appears a bell at either side. *Cf.* A48.

A36. Elephant (height $1' 2\frac{3}{4}''$) with traces of rider and servant probably from the East Gateway (lowest architrave; north end). Mouth, forehead and legs missing. The details are treated in the same way as in A35, but the *uttara chhada* is plain and the bell on the right is broken.

A37. Figure of a winged lion ($2' 1\frac{3}{4}''$) in three pieces. Mouth, ears, tops of wings and portions of fore-legs missing; left leg restored in plaster of Paris. The mane and wings are conventionally treated. *Cf.* lions surmounting the jambs of the South Gateway.

A38—A41. Mutilated figures of four winged lions. Legs, tops of wings, face of A39 and heads of A38, A40 and A41 missing. Details treated in the same way as in A37. Heights, $1' 4''$; $1' 4\frac{3}{4}''$; $1'$; and $1' 1\frac{1}{4}''$.

A42. Branch of a mango tree (height 1′ ¾″ ; width 8″) from one of the small supports between the projecting ends of architraves.

A43. Tree with a small weather-worn *yakshi* from the projecting end of an architrave. Height 1′ 4¾″ ; width 11″. The tree is similar to A25. Of the *yakshi* figure, arms from shoulders and legs below knees are missing. The *dhoti* is fastened by a girdle tied in knot at the left hip. The hair and dress are treated in the same way as in A26.

A44. Section of a small tree (height 10¾″ ; width 1′ 5¼″) with the left arm of a *yakshi* figure wearing bangles and armlets. The tree is similar to A25. The fragment was broken across the middle.

A45. Fragment (height 9¾″) of a small bracket tree. The leaves of the tree resemble the petals of a full blown flower.

A46. Upper part of a short baluster (height 1′ 1½″ ; width 6¼″) from between the architraves of a gateway. On front portion of palmette in the central position and a lotus flower above. The carving on the back has disappeared. The sides are rough dressed.

A47. Top portion of a similar baluster (height 1′ 1½″). Front relieved with capital of a pillar surmounted by four lions set back to back and supporting a *chakra*.

A48. Elephant (height 1′ 6¾″ ; length 1′ 3½″) with rider and servant from between the architraves of a gateway. Lower part of trunk and legs missing. Plain *uttara chhada*. Rider on neck driving the elephant ; servant seated with doubled legs on the back of the animal. The servant holds the faggot shaped staff of a waving flag ending in a *nandipada* symbol at the top. The elephant is carved in the round in the normal way, but the riders have double bodies above the loins and were made to face both ways. Mark the prominence of the elephant's skull. (Pl. X)

A49. Elephant (height 11⅝″) with remnants of rider and servant probably from between the lowest and middle architraves of the North Gateway. Trunk and legs missing and right eye damaged. *Uttara chhada* treated in the same way as in A48. The two ropes fastened to the girth probably supported the servants' seat.

A50. Elephant (height 1′ 1½″) with remnants of rider and servant from between the architraves of a gateway. The plain *uttara chhada* is treated in the same way as in A44. A goad (*aṅkuśa*) is placed on the elephant's head. Found in 1917-18, outside the circuit wall to the east of the Museum.

A51. Mutilated figure (height 1′ 2″) of a horseman with part of back and neck of the horse from between the architraves of a gateway. Like the riders in A48, this rider has also a double body above the loins.

A52. Broken trident (height 3′ 7¼″; width 2′ 2¾″) from the top of the South, East or West Gateway of Stupa I. Pieced together from seven fragments and much mutilated.

A53. Torso (height 1′ 8¼″) of a *chaurī* bearer from one of the gateways. Wears elaborate pearl-and-stone necklace and a *dhoti* fastened by a plain girdle of which the ends are hanging in front. Remnants of scarf at the back.

A54. Damaged torso (height 1′ 4½″) of a *chaurī* bearer from a gateway. Scarf ; remnants of necklace above the navel ; *dhoti* fastened by a plain band and a scarf.

A55. Head (height 10½″) of a *chaurī* bearer wearing large jewelled ear-pendants and Indian turban with a high top-knot in front and another over the skull. Three folds on the neck. Found in debris near the North Gateway.

E

A56. Fragment (height $1\frac{1}{2}''$) of a wheel (*chakra*) from a gateway. Traces of spokes on the inner face.

A57. Mutilated torso (height 11″) of a double-bodied *yaksha* wearing *dhoti* and ornaments.

A58. Fragment (height $10\frac{1}{2}''$) of the legs of a double-bodied *yaksha* standing. The *dhoti* was fastened by a girdle the embroidered ends of which are falling in front. To judge by its size, the figure must have served as a *chaurī* bearer; but the exact provenance cannot be ascertained.

A59. Fragment (height 10″) of a small bracket with feet of a *yakshi* figure wearing heavy anklets. Rough dressed at back.

A60. Fragment (height $8\frac{1}{2}''$) of a small bracket (?) with the left foot of *yakshi* wearing heavy anklets. A *yakshi* in the North Gateway of Stupa I wears such heavy anklets, and A59 and A60 might also have belonged to the gateways.

Fragments belonging to gateways other than those of Stupa I and Stupa III.

A61. Upright (height 2′ $1\frac{1}{4}''$; width $9\frac{1}{4}''$; thickness $10\frac{1}{2}''$) from between the architraves of a gateway. Grey sandstone. The front face is relieved with a standing male figure wearing *dhoti*, ornaments and head-dress with three top-knots. On either side of the figure, garlands suspended on pegs. Floral design at black. The sides are rough dressed.

A62. Upright (height 1′ $9\frac{1}{4}''$; width $10\frac{1}{2}''$) similar to A61. On front, the *sambodhi*, or enlightenment of the Buddha represented by a throne placed under a garlanded *pipal* tree, which is surmounted by an umbrella also decorated with garlands. On the back, a floral design.

A63. Upper part of a bracket (height $9\frac{3}{4}''$; width $10\frac{1}{2}''$) of white grey sandstone. Front face relieved with the branches of a mango tree with one of the branches held in the left hand of a *yakshi*. The back and sides are rough dressed.

Stupa II.

Small portions of the berm and stairway railings of Stupa II (A64—A66) have been reconstructed with the help of the original pieces and set up in the Museum. The pillars from the stairway railing (A65-A66) are carved both on the front and back; those from the berm railing (A64) only on the front, the back being quite plain with the exception of small donatory inscriptions on pillars *a*, *b*, *d*, and *h*. As a rule, the pillars of a berm railing were generally ornamented on the outer face, the inner side—facing the stupa—being left plain. In A64, however, the order has been reversed because the plain faces of the pillars would have been of little or no interest to visitors.

A64. Eight pillars have been used in the section of the berm railing. The average height of the restored pillars is 3′ 1″ each.

(*a*) The corner pillar at the north end is carved on 3 sides. The decoration on the front face contains a dwarfish *yaksha* near the top, riding a monster with the fore-part of a bull and the body and tail of a fish, the rider holding a horn of the monster in his right hand and the fish-tail in his left. Above the floral decoration on the outer side is a parrot holding a flower in its beak. On the back is a Persepolitan column surmounted by a wheel (*chakra*) above which is a Prākṛit inscription of two lines in archaic Brāhmī characters reading :—

L. 1. *Para*................

L. 2. *Nagasenasa*....[*da*]............

Pillar (*b*). In 3 pieces. Half lotus in the upper, and lower and full lotus in the central medallion. Inscription at back reads :—

L. 1. *Ajanāvā Āvāsi*

L. 2. *kasa dānaṁ*

= "The gift of Āvāsika from Anjnāvā."[1]

Pillar (*c*). Half lotus below and legs of elephant in the middle.

Pillar (*d*). Lotuses in the lower and central medallions. Brāhmī inscription at back reads :—

L. 1. *Visakasa Rohanipadiyasa*

L. 2. *dāna*

= "The gift of Visaka (Visvaka), the inhabitant of Rohanipada.'

Pillar (*e*). Half lotus in the lower and figure of a bull in the central disc.

Pillar (*f*). Upper half. Palmette in the central disc ; lotus in the upper.

Pillar (*g*). Lower half. Lotuses in the lower and central medallions.

Pillar (*h*). Corner pillar at the south end. Floral decoration on front, surmounted by an elephant, above which is an umbrella. Brāhmī inscription on the back reading :—

Idadatasa upāsakasa dāna

= "The gift of the lay-worshipper Idadata (Indradatta)"[2]

A65. Small section of the stairway railing of Stupa II, consisting of three pillars standing on a sloping kerb-stone. The pillars are relieved with lotus designs on the front and back. The kerb-stone is the only one of its kind found near Stupa II.

A66. Four fragmentary pillars and a long kerb-stone from the railing of the stairway landing of Stupa II, partially restored. Length 5′ 6″. Originally this section of the berm railing consisted of six pillars. The lower halves of the pillars (*a*) and (*b*), the top and bottom portions of (*c*) and the upper half of (*d*) have been restored.

Pillar (*a*).—The carving on the front is divided into three compartments one above the other. The top panel contains a sixteen spoked wheel, possibly representing the first sermon of the Buddha at Sārnāth. The second panel contains three male figures, who support the wheel in the upper compartment with their right uplifted hands and carry some indistinct objects—(fruit ?) — in their left. Below them in the lowest panel, is a banyan tree. The left or outer face of the pillar is decorated with a floral design below and the birth scene of Buddha above, the latter represented by a figure of Māya standing on a full blown lotus and being bathed by two elephants holding water pots in their trunks.

Pillar (*b*).—The birth scene of the Buddha on the front and back. Above the carving at the back, which is badly damaged, is a Prākṛit inscription in archaic Brāhmī characters reading :—

[*Si*] *harakhitasa bhichhuno dānaṁ*

"The gift of the monk Siharakhita."

[1] Bühler, *E. I.*, II, p. 399, No. 43 ; Luder's *List*, No. 619.

[2] Bühler, *E. I.*, II, p. 399, No. 45 ; Luder's *List*, No. 621.

Pillar (*c*).—The old piece is made up of three small fragments. The relief on the front contains a damaged elephant in the central medallion and remnants of a floral design below. Traces of a floral pattern at back.

Pillar (*d*).—Half lotus below and floral design above, both on the front and outer faces. Observe the straight stalk of the plant on the outer face with blossoms arranged one above the other.

Stupa III.

A67. Lid (length 2′ ½″; width 2′ 1½″) of a relic-box of buff grey sandstone from Stupa III. On the top is a Brāhmī inscription of one line reading :—

Mahāmogalānasa

i.e. " [The relics] of Mahāmogalāna (Mahāmaudgalyāna)."

A68. Similar lid from Stupa III, in two pieces (1′ 8″×11¼″ and 1′ 11½″×1′ 2″). Some fragments of lid missing. On top, traces of a Brāhmī inscription reading :—

[*Sā*] [*ri*] [*pu*] [*ta*] [*sa*]
i.e. "[The relics of] Sāriputa (Sāriputra)."

Mahāmogalāna and Sāriputra were among the chief disciples and companions of the Buddha. But the stupa belongs to the Śuṅga period. These relics must, therefore, have had some other resting place or places before they were transferred to this stupa.

Sculptures of the Early School.

A69. Coping (length 5′ 7″) of buff grey sandstone probably from the harmikā railing of Stupa IV. Decorated on face with an undulating lotus design with birds perched in the foliage. About 2nd century B.C. (Pl. XI)

A70. Fragment (height 8¼″; width 6¼″) of a railing pillar of buff grey sandstone carved on three sides. The relief on front contains lotus buds and flowers above, and bust of a human figure wearing ornaments and elaborate head-dress below. On the right side are sprinkled a number of small lotus flowers above which are the feet of a male and a female figure to right and two letters of a Brāhmī inscription reading "*hika*" to left. The left face of the pillar is ornamented with a lotus design enclosed by a bead and reel decoration. (Pl. IV)

A71. Fragment (height 1′ ½″; width 8″) of an inscribed railing pillar of light grey sandstone decorated with a well modelled figure of a spirited he-goat standing in the central medallion. Below the figure is an inscription of two lines in archaic Brāhmī characters, reading :—

1. *Vasumitasa bhaya* [*ye*]
2. *Poṭhi* [*ni*] *yā*

"[The gift] of Poṭhini (Prosṭhinī) wife of Vasumitra." (Pl. VII)

A72. Fragment (height 7¼″; width 6½″) of a railing pillar of buff grey sandstone with remnants of a horseman in the central medallion. Below the figure is a fragmentary inscription of one line in archaic Brāhmī characters, reading :— ..*vasa Kaṭakañu*......

A73. Fragment (height 6¾″ ; width 11″) of an octagonal pillar of dark purplish sandstone with remnants of undulating lotus design on front. The leaves are given the peculiar turn which is a characterestic of the floral decorations of the Early School.

A74. Fragment (height 4¾″; width 7½″) of a railing pillar of buff red sandstone. Remnants of a floral decoration on the front face above and an inscription of one line in archaic Brāhmī characters below. The inscription reads :—

Arahadāsiya dāna

"The gift of Arahadāsi."

A75. Top portion (height 10¼″ ; width 8¼″) of a baluster of dark grey sandstone from the stairway railing of a stupa. Half lotus in the top medallion ; below the lotus, inscription of one line in early Brāhmī characters reading :—

L. 1. Sonanadēva [*sa*]

L. 2. [*dāna*]

"The gift of Sonadēva."

A76. Lower half (height 10¼″ ; width 4½″) of a small corner pillar from the berm railing of a stupa decorated with lotuses on two sides.

A77. Small cross-bar (length 7″ ; height 4½″) probably belonging to the same balustrade as A76. On front, inscription of two lines in later Brāhmī characters, reading :—

L. 1. Mūl[*ā*]*ya bhikuni*

L. 2. yā dānaṁ

"The gift of the nun Mūla...." Found from debris of Stupa 5.

A78. Similar cross-bar (7″ × 4½″) with inscription reading :—

L. 1. Kaṇhamitasa dānaṁ

L. 2. yo

"The gift of Kaṇhamita (Krishṇamitra)." Found in the debris of Temple 40.

A79. Fragment (length 1′ 3¼″ ; height 5″ ; width 4⅝″) of a coping stone from the berm railing of the same stupa as Nos. A76—78.

A80. Fragment (length 1′ ; height 5¼″ ; width 4⅞″) of a coping stone probably from the harmikā railing of the same stupa as Nos. A76—79. The face is ornamented with an undulating lotus design.

A81. Statue of a lion (length 3′ 5″ ; height 2′ 4¾″) in the round. Grey sandstone. Head, legs and tail missing, and hips damaged. It was found about 50 yards to the N. W. of Stupa II, and might have served as the crowning member of the column some pieces of which are still lying near that stupa. About 2nd-3rd century A.D.

Sculptures of the Kushān and Gupta Schools.

A82. Statue (height 1′ 6¼″ ; width 1′ 3⅝″) of Bodhisattva seated in the *dhyānamudrā*. Mathurā sandstone. Head, arms and knees missing. Wears necklaces and an amulet cord on right side with two amulets attached. Right shoulder bare, folds of garment over left ;

scarf round the loins. End of *dhoti* and tassels of girdle falling on the seat below the legs. Inscription of three lines in Brāhmī characters of the Kushān period on pedestal reads :—

L. 1. ....sya [rā] *j*[*ā*] *t*[*i*] *r* [*ā*] *jasya Dēvaputrasya sh*[*ā*]*hi V*[*ā*]*s*[*ī*]*shkasya sa* [*ṁ*] *20 8 he 1 di 5 as ya purv* [*āyāṁ*] *Bhaga*[*va*]

L. 2. sya jambuchhāyā-śailagṛi [*ha*]*sya*[1] *Dharmadēva vihārē pratishṭāpita Virasya dhitare Madhuriaka*

L. 3. [*Anē*]*na deyadharma-pari* [*tyāgena*].......

"Success: In the year 28 of Mahārāja Rājātirāja Devaputra Shāhi Vāsishka, in the first month of winter, on the fifth day, on this date, Madhurikā, daughter of Vīra, installed (an image) of Bhagavat (Bodhisattva) sitting on the hill under the shade of the Jambu (rose-apple) tree in the Dharmadāvavihāra. By this gift........."

Jambhuchhāyāśailagṛihasya evidently refers to the miracle that Buddha as Prince Siddhārtha performed under a Jambu-tree at the time of the "Ploughing Festival." On that occasion king Śuddhodana with his son and a large retinue went to the field and made the prince Siddhārtha seat under a Jambu-tree on a couch (*asyanam*) with a canopy inlaid with stars of gold over it and a curtain hung around. Siddhārtha, finding himself alone, sat cross-legged and sank into spiritual meditation (*dhyāna*). "The shadows of the other trees turned round, but that of the Jambu tree remained steady and circular in form."[2]

A slightly different version of the story is given in the Lalita Vistara[3], and the place where Siddhārtha sat under the Jambu-tree is called Kṛishi-grāmagiri, "the hill in the village of the ploughmen."[4] (Pl. II)

A83. Pedestal with feet (1′ 4″×11½″) of a standing image of Buddha. Mathurā sandstone. Between the feet is an uncertain object; to proper left, the feet of a smaller attendant figure. The front face of the pedestal is relieved by a dentil cornice above and a Persopolitan pilaster at either side. In the centre of the panel is a Bodhisattva wearing elaborate head-dress and ornaments and seated cross-legged in the *dhyānamudrā*. To the right of the Bodhisattva are six male worshippers, to the left five female. The male figures, both men and boys, wear long tunics of the typical Kushān type, held in with a belt above the hips. The females wear *sāris* and bodices. Some of the worshippers carry lotuses and other offerings; others hold their hands in the attitude of prayer. On the pedestal is an inscription in Brāhmī characters of the Kushān period reading as follows :—

L. 1. ....*rājño Vasṇushāṇasya sa 20 2 va 2 di 10 Bhagavato Sakkyam* [*un*]*e ḥ pratimā pratishṭāpit* [*a*] *Vidyamatiy* [*e*] *pa*

L. 2. ....*yya mātā-pitṛiṇa sarvvasattanā cha su* i.e. "In the year 22 of King Vasṇushāṇa in the second month of the rainy season, on the 10th day, the image of the Bhagavat Sākyamuni was installed by Vidyāmatī....for the happiness of the donor's parents and of all creatures."

[1] Dr. Vogels' reading *Jambuchhāca for Jambuchhāyā* is probably a misprint. *Ya* is quite clear on Bühler's plate (E. I. Vol. II, pl. facing p. 368) as well as on the stone.

[2] The Nidānakathā (Rhys Davids, *Buddhist Birth Stories*, London, 1880, p. 74*f*; Fausbell, *The Jatakas*, Vol. I, p. 57*f*.

[3] Lefmann, *Lalita Vistara*, Chapter XI, pp. 128-36.

[4] For a Gandhara sculpture excavated at Sahri-Bahlol representing prince Siddhārtha seated under the Jambu-tree see A. S. R., 1911-12, Pt. II, p. 190, Plate XL, fig. 12. The figure of a ploughman at the base places the identification beyond doubt.

The sculpture is a product of the Mathurā school which flourished about the 2nd century A.D. under the Kushāns. The name of the King Vasṇushāṇa is, however, a strange one and we might recognise in him a foreigner who probably came into power in and around Mathurā after the fall of Vasudeva Kushān. (Pl. XII)

A84. Fragment of a pedestal (8″×7¾″) with remnants of the left foot of a standing image wearing sandals. Mathurā sandstone. To right of pedestal, stunted pilaster with foliated cap ; in sunk panel, a partly mutilated figure of the Bodhisattva Maitreya seated cross-legged and holding a small flask in the left hand. To left of the Bodhisattva, two female devotees clad in *sāris* each holding lotus stalk in right hand, and hem of *sāri* in left. On the raised borders above and below the panel is engraved an inscription of three lines in Brāhmī characters of the Kushān period :—

L. 1. (above the panel)........*[Bodhi] satvasya Maitrēyasya pratimā pratishṭ [ā]*
L. 2. (below the panel)........*sya kuṭumbini yē Vishākulasya dhitu Vadi*
L. 3. (below the panel)........*tana[hi] [ta] sukh[ā]rtha[m]bhavatu*

"The image of the Bodhisattva Maitreya has been installed by................ the relative of........daughter of Vishakula..........May it be for the welfare and happiness of "[1]

Found in the fallen masonry of the relic chamber of Stupa 12.

A84. (*a*) Small fragment (2⅞″×1⅜″) from A84 with the big and second toe of the right foot of a figure wearing sandals. Mathurā sandstone. One complete and 2 broken letters of inscription on the pedestal.

A84. (*b*) Fragment (height 3¾″×2¼″) from the left side of A84. Relieved with the figure of an attendant wearing tunic and carrying a garland. The inscription on the pedestal has chipped off.

A85. Votive tablet (Āyāgapaṭa) of Mathurā sandstone (11¼″×8½″). Broken on all four sides and impressed with a (?) foot-print of which the heel only remains. The heel is ornamented with a *nandipada* symbol countersunk in relief and traces of quatrefoil flowers remain on the border. Between the floral border and the heel, is a donatory inscription in early Gupta characters. It is sadly disfigured and seems to record that the tablet was the gift of an *upāsaka* (whose name is not clear on the stone) for one Jeṭhagupta.

A86. Fragment (length 10½″ ; height 4¾″) of a pedestal with toes of the right foot of a standing figure. Mathurā sandstone. On the face of the pedestal is an inscription of three lines in the Northern variety of Gupta characters :—

L. 1. jālāṅgulir-dīpta suvarṇa g [au raḥ]
— — ◡ — — ∨ ∨ — ◡ — —.[1]
— — ◡ — — ∨ ∨ — ◡ — —
[cha]
L. 2. ndromayukhai-riva gharma taptān [II] tasya triloka th. (?)
L. 3. lenaśaila hēmojvalā śmarakulātmajēna....

The inscription consisted of two stanzas, the first of which was in the *Indravajrā* metre. To judge from the remnants of the epigraph, it appears to have recorded the dedication of the image by one who claimed to belong to Śmarakula, *i.e.*, the line of Pradyumna, son of Krishna, and therefore to a branch of the Yādava race.

[1] A. S. R., 1913-14, pt. II, p. 16 ; Sir John Marshall, *Guide to Sanchi*, p. 86. For a photograph of the pedestal see A. S. R., 1912-13, Pt. I, Pl. VIII(*b*).

A87. Image (height 1′8″) of Buddha standing with right knee slightly bent. Mathurā sandstone. Head, feet and right arm missing; chest and left hand slightly injured. *Saṅghāṭī* covers both shoulders and arms; the lower garment shows above the ankles. The left hand holds the upper garment at hip; the right was apparently disposed in the *abhayamudrā*. Early Gupta.

A88. Torso (height 11½″) of Buddha erect. Mathurā sandstone. Head, hands and legs below knees missing. *Saṅghāṭī* covers both shoulders and arms. The right hand was evidently raised in the attitude of imparting security (*abhayamudrā*). Early Gupta.

A89. Fragmentary pedestal (height 6¾″; width 9¼″) with the left shin and right foot of a Buddha figure seated cross-legged. Mathurā sandstone. Wheel symbol on the heel and *triratna* mark on the sole of right foot. The drapery is carved in folds.

A90. Fragment (7¼″×5½″) from the pedestal of a Buddhist statue representing a standing male figure in monkish robes. Mathurā sandstone. Feet missing. Head clean-shaved. Garland and lotuses in the right hand which is raised to the shoulder; and offerings in the left which is placed on the navel. Late Kushān.

A91. Fragment (height 7″; width 5¼″) from the left side of a Buddhist sculpture of Mathurā sandstone representing a standing figure of a male devotee. Head, left arm from shoulder and legs below knees missing. Wears *dhoti* and ornaments; and like the figure in A90, carries a garland and lotuses in the right hand and offerings in the left. Late Kushān.

A92. Fragment (height 9¾″; width 7⅝″) of a halo of Mathurā sandstone with several concentric bands of ornament. The central portion contains traces of lotus design enclosed by a beaded border. The next pattern consists of spear-shaped rays radiating towards the outer edge. The carving of the next band resembles a metallic chain adorned with lotus-marked discs strewn at regular intervals. This again is surrounded by a string of beads after which we find the usual scalloped border. Gupta.

A93. Fragment (1′ 8″×4¾″) of a halo of Mathurā sandstone decorated in the same way as A92. Gupta.

A94. Fragment (width 1′ 1¼″×height 1′ ½″) of a richly sculptured halo of grey sandstone. Lotus design in centre, surrounded by two concentric bands of delicately carved floral and foliated patterns, in which the leaves assume the appearance of scrolls, enclosed in their turn, by a leaf ornament. The fragment belongs to the halo of the Dhyāni Buddha statue placed against the terrace wall opposite the South Gateway of Stupa I, but owing to the nature of the breakage cannot be fitted. Gupta.

A95. * Relief (height 2′ 7″; width 2′ 11″) of grey sandstone in 3 pieces representing Buddha with a female attendant on left and male on right, each holding a flask on left hip. Head of Buddha broken and hands damaged. Right shoulder bare. Right hand holds drapery at shoulder, left pointing towards a kneeling devotee who has spread his hair on the ground for the Buddha to tread on. Early Gupta.

A96. Square capital (height 11½″×1′ 4″×1′ 4″) of a pilaster provided with a hole in the centre and a large tenon at the bottom. Grey sandstone. The decoration on the front

* This relief has since been removed from the museum and placed in front of the Antiquity godown to north of that building. Possibly it represented the story of the Dipaṅkara Buddha.

consists of a *yaksha* figure at each corner and a lotus plant in the middle. Similar plant designs at the sides. The back and portions of sides are plain. Early Gupta. (Pl. XI)

A97. Square capital (height 1′ 1½″×15¼″×15¼″) of a column similar to the preceding one. Relieved with *yakshas* and plants on all four sides. Early Gupta.

A98. Inscribed stone (length 2′ 6″; ht. 9″) from Kānākheṛa, near Sāñchī, where it was used in a well. Dark grey sandstone. The inscription is written in Brāhmī characters of the Gupta period. The language is Sanskrit. A considerable portion of the epigraph is defaced. It records the digging of a well by one Mahādandanāyaka Śaka Śridharavarmman, son of Śaka Nanda.

A99. Standing statue (height 5′ 1½″) of the Bodhisattva Vajrapāṇi from the top of the Gupta column in front of the North Gateway of Stupa I. Grey sandstone. Arms from shoulders and legs below knees missing. Wears richly jewelled necklace, heavy ear-rings and elaborate head-dress of *kīrtimukha* heads, swags and jewels. The head-dress is much damaged. The hair is arranged in three rows of ringlets and falls over the shoulders and back; and beneath it at the back fall ends of two ribands. The short *dhoti* is fastened with an ornamented girdle tied in knot. The right hand appears to have held a *vajra* of which one of the trident ends is still traceable on the right hip; the left hand held ends of scarf on the left hip. The halo, which is evidently too small in proportion to the size of the statue, is pierced with twelve holes evenly disposed around its edge. These holes were apparently intended for receiving ends of the outer rays "which were probably fashioned out of copper gilt, the rest of the statue itself being possibly painted or gilded."[1] The figure was broken across the middle. Early Gupta.

A100. Statue (height 8′ 0″) of the Bodhisattva Padmapāṇi standing with left knee slightly bent. Grey sandstone. Wears elaborate tiara, ornaments, scarf and a short *dhoti*. The right uplifted hand holds a lotus (*padma*) against the shoulder; the left an end of scarf on hip. In front of the tiara is a *kīrtimukha* head spouting forth garlands. The *dhoti* is fastened by a plain girdle tied in front and the ends of the scarf are hanging in folds at the left side. The halo is rather peculiar and it appears that the rays of metal in No. A99 were here probably painted on the plain nimbus. Beneath the pedestal of the statue is a projecting tenon for mortice. About 4th century A.D.

A101. Statue (height 7′ 6″) of the Bodhisattva Padmapāṇi similar in all respects to the one described above. The right knee is slightly bent. The details are not so well preserved.

A102. Statue (height 6′ 10″) in three pieces of a standing Nāga figure with seven-headed serpent-hood above the head and serpent coils at the back and sides. Reddish grey sandstone. Wears tiara, *dhoti* and scarf. The right uplifted hand holds a full blown lotus; the left, a flask on hip. From each of the serpent mouths come out bifurcated tongues. In front of the tiara is a *kīrtimukha* head spouting forth swags. The *dhoti* is fastened by a plain girdle tied in front. The scarf shows in front of the knees and over the left arm with its ends hanging at the left side. Early Gupta. (Pl. I)

A103. Statue (height 6′ 7½″) in three pieces of a standing Nāga figure of buff grey sandstone wearing similar dress and ornaments as A102. Serpent-hoods broken; tiara and features of the face badly damaged. The hands rest on hips: the right, holding a *padma* and two lotus buds; the left, a flask. A lion head in the centre of each face of the tiara is spouting forth

[1] Sir John Marshall, *Guide to Sañchi*, p. 99.

D

garlands. The ends of the scarf are hanging at the sides and a long garland appears on the arms and in front of the knees. Early Gupta.

A104. Figure (height 1′ 3½″; length 2′ 1½″; width 1′ 6½″) in high relief of a double lion seated with the right fore-paw placed on the left. It has two separate bodies, but only one head and four legs. Gupta.

Four other lions of a similar type, but three of them smaller in dimensions and all more or less mutilated, are placed in the Antiquity godown attached to the Museum. They were probably used as capitals of pilasters and were meant to be seen on two sides.

A105. Statue (height 1′ 8″) of Buddha seated in European fashion on a throne supported by two lions. Buff brown sandstone. Left arm, right fore-arm, and left leg missing; hands mutilated; face damaged. The *ushṇīsha* is ornamented. The right shoulder is bare. The hands were disposed in the attitude of preaching. The figure was broken across the middle. About 5th century A.D.

A106. Inscribed pedestal (width 1′ 8″, ht. 8″) with traces of feet of a standing figure. Dark-purplish sandstone. The inscription consists of one line written in characters of the Gupta period and reads :—

> *deyadharmoyaṁ bhadanta* [*R*] *ekhaguptasya yadatra-puṇyaṁ ta* [*dbha*]......
>
> "This is the pious gift of the Reverend Rekhagupta. Let the merit of this (deed) accrue (to all creatures)."

Sculptures of the Later Mediæval period.

A107. Broken oval halo (height 1′ 3⅜″; width 1′ 4¾″) of buff sandstone in three pieces. Central portion quite plain and surrounded by a narrow band inscribed with a part of the Buddhist creed in acute-angled characters of about the 7th-8th century A.D. Beyond this, a band of beautiful foliated design surrounded by a string of beads. The inscription reads :—

> ......*prabhahā hetuṁ teshāṁ Tathāgato hyavadat=teshāṁ cha yo* [*niro*] *dha evāṁvādī*......

A108. Statue of a lion (height 1′ 8″; length 2′ 6½″) of grey sandstone. Head detached but refixed; face, legs and tail missing; chest partially mutilated; back slightly damaged in two places where the tail touched the body. On the haunches and shoulders are four trident shaped locks of hair. On the left hip is an inscription in characters of about the 8th century A.D. The inscription is badly damaged and the few letters that can be read yield no sense.

A109. Head in relief (1′ 2¼″×1′ 1″) of the Bodhisattva Avalokiteśvara. Grey sandstone. Nose, lips and earlobes damaged. Wears a high head-dress with a short projection at either side. Above the head-dress is a damaged effigy of the Dhyāni Buddha Amitābha in meditation. The black slab is pointed at the top.

A110. Statue (height 1′ 4″) of Jambhāla seated in the easy posture (*līlāsana*) on an ornamental seat supported on five vases. Dark purplish sandstone. Head, right hand and knee missing; left hand and foot damaged. Wears ornaments. The right foot rests on two reversed vases. The left hand, placed on the knee, holds a mongoose. On the breast is a shallow mark resembling the *śrivatsa* symbol (Pl. XIII)

A111. Head-less statue (height 1' 11") of a female deity, probably Tārā, standing on inverted lotus. Dark purplish sandstone. Right fore-arm missing; left hand damaged; right breast mutilated. Wears ornaments. The left hand, raised to the shoulder, holds stalk of lotus springing from a flower-pot placed near the left knee of the goddess. The right hand was apparently held in the gift-bestowing attitude. Encircling the arms and hanging from them, what might be the ends of a scarf.

A112. Four-armed figure of (?) Śiva (height 1' ½") wearing ornaments and seated in the easy posture (*līlāsana*) on a double lotus throne supported by a bull. Upper arms missing; left foot broken. Lower right hand in *abhayamudrā*; left holds vase (*kamaṇḍalu*) on pedestal below the left knee. (?) Lotus stalk turned round right leg and appearing in front of right shoulder, also round lower left arm. (Pl. XIII)

A photograph of this sculpture was circulated to several members of the Archæological Department for identification. Mr. Bhandarkar suggested that it might represent Harihara, Mr. Krishna Shastri suggested its identity with Dattātreya and the late Mr. Natesa Aiyar thought that it might be a Nīlakaṇṭhāryāvalōkiteśvāra or Hālāhala Lokeśvara. Mr. Banerji, on the other hand, was sure that it was Śiva; and Mr. Hargreaves could not think of its being anything else. None of these identifications was convincing to the late Mr. Panday who was inclined to think that the figure was probably a Jaina conception of Śiva.

Rai Bahadur Daya Ram Sahni has found some images of Siva at Sārnāth which are very similar to the figure in question in style and execution and belong to the late Mediæval period. The Rai Bahadur is of opinion that this figure must also be a representation of Śiva. It was brought to the Museum from the Madāgan tank near Sāñchī. About 11th century A.D. (Pl. XIII)

A113. Fragment (height 8½"; width 10¼") from the upper left hand corner of a sculpture of buff-brown sandstone representing a damaged dwarfish *gandharva* flying in clouds to left, and head of *makara* spouting forth a scroll design to right, with remnants of halo above. The *gandharva* carries an open garland with forked ends and wears necklace, girdle and high boots, but apparently no under-garment.

A114. Fragment (height 9½"; width 6¼") of halo and right hand *gandharva* figure from the same sculpture as No. A113; but the *gandharva* is better preserved.

A115. Damaged *yaksha* (height 11¼") of dark-purplish sandstone. Back slab broken and head, feet and left arm missing. The figure is apparently nude but wears necklace, girdle and wristlets, the girdle being ornamented with curious circular pendants (bells ?). The right hand holds a spherical object against the breast.

A116. Fragment (8¼"×8¼") from the upper right hand corner of a sculpture representing a flying garland-bearing *gandharva* in clouds. Dark purplish sandstone. From building 32, debris.

A117. Fragment (height 6¼"; width 5¾") from the upper left corner of a sculpture with remnants of halo and garland-bearing *gandharva* and *gandharvini* on clouds. Dark purplish sandstone. The *gandharvini* is seated on the legs of her male companion. In her right hand she holds a stalk of lotus; the left is raised up with the palm turned towards the face.

A118. Fragment (height 1' 4½"; width 7½") of a stele of dark-purplish sandstone divided into two vertical compartments. In the upper panel, a naked ascetic and a well-dressed lay worshipper standing; in the lower, remnants of two worshippers.

A119. Fragment (height 6½"; width 6½") of a stele of dark-purplish sandstone relieved with a roaring lion. The tail of the lion is raised and carried along the back.

A120. Pedestal with legs and fore-arms of a (?) Bodhisattva figure seated cross-legged on a damaged lotus throne (height 5¾"; width 7⅜".) Dark-purplish sandstone. Wears wristlets. The left hand, on knee, holds stalk of lotus; the right is in the gift-bestowing attitude. On either side of the figure, traces of an attendant standing on lotus. On pedestal fragment of an inscription of two lines in cursive Nāgarī characters of the late Mediæval period.

A121. Pedestal with legs and hands of a Bodhisattva figure seated in the easy posture on a double lotus throne supported by two lions. (height 8½"; width 9½"). Buff-red sandstone. Wears girdle and anklets. The right hand is held in the *varadamudrā,* the left holds stalk of lotus springing from the pedestal. To right of the Bodhisattva, attendant in devotional attitude.

A122. Fragment (height 9¾"; width 11½") of a sculpture of buff-red sandstone. Above zig-zag decoration to left and lion's head in a circular niche to right; below, damaged head, of a demoniac *yaksha* with moustaches, curly hair and beard and long canine teeth. The tongue of the *yaksha* is pressed between his lips and in his right ear lobe, he wears a large round ear button.

A123. Figure (height 9½"; width 6⅝") of four-armed Gaṇēśa seated on a cushion in the easy posture. Buff-red sandstone. Halo behind the head. The upper right hand holds a rosary; the lower, an uncertain object, perhaps a flower. In the upper left hand the god holds an *aṅkuśa*; in the lower, a vessel of round cakes which he is picking up with his trunk. The sacred thread is marked on the chest and belly.

A124. Pedestal with elongated lotus bud and remnants of the left foot of a standing figure. Buff-red sandstone. Height 1' 5½"; width 1' 0". On the pedestal, kneeling female worshipper. Along the right margin of the slab is a fragment of inscription in Nāgarī characters of the late Mediæval period; but no sense can be made out. Found in debris of building 20.

A125. Fragmentary pedestal (height 1' 4") and feet of a deity standing on lotus. Elongated lotus bud to left with a *preta* squatting in front with hands upraised to receive the drops of nectar (*amrita*) flowing from the fingers of the deity's right hand. Along the left margin of the slab, inscription of one line in Nāgarī characters of about the 12th century A.D. containing a fragment of the Buddhist creed.

A126. Fragment (height 1' 3¼"; width 6") of a sculpture of dark purplish sandstone bearing an elongated lotus bud and the right fore-arm of a female figure wearing a broad bracelet. The hand rests on the lotus bud. Along the left margin is a fragmentary inscription of two lines in Nāgarī characters of about the 12th century A.D.; but no sense can be made out.

A127. Broken pedestal (height 5½"; length 1' 5½") with toes of the right foot of an image of dark purplish sandstone. On the face of the pedestal, lotus and beautiful scroll work.

B—Antiquities in the South Room.

B1. Bowl of dark purplish sandstone pieced together from several fragments and partially restored. Diameter 1′ 8″; height 9⅓″. On the rim of the bowl is a Prākṛit inscription of one line in archaic Brāhmī characters reading *Bhāgāya pasādō, i.e.*, " for the distribution of food (offered at the shrine)."

The fragments of the bowl were discovered near the bottom of a heap of *debris*, in the angle formed by the retaining wall to the west of Temple 18, and the wall at right angles to it along the south face of the central plateau. Much of this accumulation of *debris* had probably fallen from the early temple terrace on the site of Temple 18. The bowl, therefore, belongs to the earlier stratum, *i.e.*, to about 3rd century B.C. as is also proved by the presence of the early Brāhmī inscription on its rim. (Pl. XIV)

Small fragments from the gateways of Stupa I.

B2. Bust (height 7″) of a double *yakshi* figure. Arms broken below the elbows; face and breasts damaged. Wears necklaces and heavy ear-pendants. Garlands are used as ornaments for the hair. (*Cf.* small *yakshi* standing on the western projection of the middle architrave of North Gateway.)

B3. Damaged head (height 4″) of a small *yakshi* wearing ear buttons.

B4. Uplifted right hand (height 5¾″) of a small *yakshi* holding a bunch of lotus buds.

B5. Middle portion (height 7½″) of the legs of a small *yakshi* wearing anklets.

B6. Fragment (height 8″) of a small tree decorated with foliage on three sides. The leaves of the tree resemble the leaves of the *Rājāyatana* tree depicted in the second panel on the front face of No. A15.

B7. Bunch of mangoes (height 5¼″) from the smaller end of the tree from beneath the lowest architrave of a gateway.

B8. Bust (height 7⅜″) of a double-faced rider. Wears Indian head-dress, necklaces and heavy ear-pendants. The rider was made to look both ways.

B9. Head (height 6¾″) of a smaller double-faced rider.

B10. Head (height 4″) of a double-faced rider. Ears and portion of head-dress missing; chin slightly injured. Part of the oblong ear-pendant sticks to the lower jaw on left. The other face is broken.

B11. Mutilated head (height 4″) of a double faced *yaksha* wearing large ear-rings and Indian head-dress with a large, high top knot in front.

B12. Damaged muzzle (height 5″) and left eye of a horse from between the architraves of a gateway. Below the eye, remnants of ornamental bridle.

B13. Fragment (height 9½″) of a bull's head probably from a false capital of a gateway. Muzzle, horns and ears missing.

B14. Head (height 6¾″) of a griffin similar to the griffins in Nos. A22 and A23. Right eye, ears and mane are slightly damaged.

B15. Front portion (width 6″) of the upper jaw of a lion representing only the nose and moustaches.

B16. Fragment (height 7½″; width 1′ 1″) of a relief from one of the gateways of Stupa I. In centre throne of Buddha placed in front of a tree of which a part of the trunk only remains.

On either side of the throne remnants of two standing devotees. Traces of a square mortice at the back.

B17. Fragment (height 5″) with legs of a standing female figure wearing heavy anklets. Traces of a railing below.

B18. Fragment (height 3½″) with waist and thighs of a standing male figure.

B19. Fragment (height 4″) from the proper right half of the head of a figure.

B20. Damaged waist and thighs of a double-bodied *yaksha*. Height 11¼″. White grey sandstone. The figure is undoubtedly a production of the Early School of Indian sculpture; but it is extremely difficult to say with certainty as to whether it belongs to any of the five gateways or not.

Sculptures of the Kushān, Gupta and Mediæval periods.

B21. Head (height 6¼″) of a Buddha figure of Mathurā sandstone. Lips, chin and left jaw broken; hair and features damaged. Traces of three folds on the neck. Kushān.

B22. Head (height 5¼″) of a female figure of white grey sandstone. Back of the left half broken and right ear damaged. Hair combed back from forehead and arranged in a chignon behind the head. The figure probably served as the right hand attendant in a group. Gupta. (Pl. XV)

B23. Left hand (length 5¾″) of a figure of Mathurā sandstone holding drapery in the palm. Fingers slightly damaged. Kushān or Gupta.

B24. Mutilated right hand (length 3¾″) of a Buddha figure of Mathurā sandstone. Little finger and tips of the other fingers broken. Wheel symbol on palm. Thumb and forefinger joined by a web which is one of the 32 superior marks (*Mahāpurusha Lakshaṇas*) of the Buddha.[1] Gupta.

B25. Left hand (4¼″×2½″) of a figure of Mathurā sandstone wearing a broad ornamental bracelet, partly concealed beneath the folds of drapery. Thumb broken and tips of fingers damaged. Wheel symbol on palm. Thumb and fore-finger joined by web. Gupta.

B26. Fragment (5¾″×4½″) of a halo of Mathurā sandstone decorated in the same way as Nos. A92 and A93. Gupta.

B27. Fragment (7¾″×5¼″) of a halo of Mathurā sandstone. Lotus design in centre surrounded by a scalloped border which is enclosed by a band of spear-shaped rays. Gupta.

B28. Fragment (4½″×3″) of a halo of white sandstone decorated in the same way as A92. Gupta.

B29. Fragment (4¼″×4″) of a halo of grey sandstone relieved with a lotus design surrounded by a band of spear-shaped rays. Gupta.

B30. Head (height 10″) of the Budhisattva Avalokiteśvara. Buff sandstone. Head-dress, tip of nose, chin and ear-lobes damaged. *Ūrṇá* at the junction of raised eyebrows. Hair in ringlets bound by a fillet with rosette in front bearing a figure of the Dhyāni Buddha Amitābha seated in the characteristic attitude of meditation. Gupta. (Pl. XV)

B31. Front portion of a Buddha head. Ht. 6¼″. Buff brown sandstone. Left eye, nose and lips slightly damaged. Hair in conventional curls. Gupta.

B32. Head (height 3¾″) of dark purplish sandstone. Back half broken; left ear lost; tip of nose damaged. Hair combed back from forehead and divided by an ornamented plait in

[1] Grunwedel, *Bud. Art in India*, p. 161.

centre. To judge by the three-quarter modelling of the face, the head seems to have belonged to an attendant figure which stood to left in a group. Gupta.

B33. Head (height 4¾") of a female figure of dark purplish sandstone. Right ear missing; left cheek and nose damaged. Hair combed back and partially arranged in short curls. *Tilaka* mark on forehead resembling a crescent and star. The figure apparently served as the right hand attendant in a group. Gupta.

B34. Head (height 5⅜") of a female figure of purplish grey sandstone. Right eye, nose, lips and chin damaged. Right ear-lobe broken; traces of ear-ring in the left. Hair combed back and arranged in a large chignon behind the head with a few ringlets in front. Gupta.

B35. Head (height 4¾") of grey sandstone. Back half of head, ears and a part of left jaw missing; face damaged. Traces of a few mutilated curls in front indicate that the hair was probably treated in the same way as in B34. Gupta.

B36. Torso (height 2¼") of a small(?) Buddha figure of grey Udayagiri sandstone. *Saṅghāṭī* covers both shoulders. The left hand holds drapery against the shoulder; the right was probably held in the attitude of charity. Late Gupta.

B37. Fragment (height 2¼"; width 2½") of pedestal with toes of the right foot of a figure of buff grey sandstone. On the face of the pedestal, remnants of an inscription of two lines in characters of the Late Kushān period, yielding no sense.

B38. Fragment (height 3"; width 5") of an inscribed pedestal with the left foot of a figure of dark purplish sandstone. The inscription consists of two lines in characters of about the 6th century A.D. and contains a fragment of the Buddhist creed.

B39. Fragment (height 5¼"; width 4") of a stele of buff grey sandstone. Carving divided into two vertical compartments. Busts of a male and a female figure in the lower compartment: the male brandishing a sword above his head, the female holding a blue lotus (*utpala*) in her left hand. The upper panel contains a fire-altar to right and traces of a figure to left. On the plain border separating the two compartments is an inscription of one line in characters of about the 5th century A.D. It is a part of the Buddhist creed and reads:—*tespāni cha yo nirodha evaṁ vādī.*

B40. Left leg and right foot of a deity seated in the easy posture on a cushion placed over a lotus flower. Height 2⅛"; width 3". Dark brown sandstone. Late Gupta.

B41. Head (height 5⅝") of a Buddha figure of buff brown sandstone. Ear-lobes and part of *ushṇīsha* missing. Mediæval.

B42. Head (height 10½"×15¼") of a figure of dark purplish sandstone with a mutilated halo behind. Ear-lobes missing; nose, eyes and lips slightly injured. Hair combed back and bound by a wreath with a small pendant in front. *Tilaka* mark on the forehead. From Temple 20, debris. Late Mediæval.

B43. Head (height 9¾") of white grey sandstone. Nose and chin damaged; right ear-lobe missing. Spiral pendant in left ear. The hair is combed back from forehead and arranged in a high triple chignon which is bound by an ornamental band with a front ornament and pendent strings of beads. Mediæval. (Pl. XV)

B44. Head (height 9⅜") of a figure of the Bodhisattva Avalokiteśvara with a mutilated halo behind. White grey sandstone. Eyes, nose and head-dress damaged. Left ear broken; remnants of ear-ring in the right. Hair arranged in a high tapering chignon with an effigy of the Dhyāni Buddha Amitābha in meditation in front. Towards the centre of the oval halo is a full blown lotus and beyond it, a recessed band of ornament containing lotus flowers. Late Mediæval. Found south of Temple 18; 2′ below surface.

B45. Mutilated bust (height 12½″) of a (?) Bodhisattva figure of buff grey sandstone with a plain oval halo behind. Right arm broken; right ear, left eyebrow, nose, lips and chin damaged. Wears ear-pendants, elaborate necklace and a peculiarly ornamented high cap. Sacred thread marked on the left shoulder and breast. Between the breasts, a diamond mark. At either side of the cap, is a short projection; and on its flat top a hemispherical knob. A recessed band of short rays connect the central portion of the halo with its outer frame. Late Mediæval.

B46. Head (height 4⅝″) of a Buddha figure of brownish grey sandstone. Ear-lobes broken; forehead, nose and lips damaged. *Ushṇīsha* on skull. Hair treated in conventional ringlets turned to right. Mediæval.

B47. Head (height 6¼″) of Avalokiteśvara. Dark purplish sandstone. Ear-lobes broken. Hair arranged in the same way as in B44 with an effigy of the Dhyāni Buddha Amitābha in front. Late Mediæval.

B48. Head (height 7⅝″) of Avalokiteśvara (?). Dark purplish sandstone. Ear-lobes missing; eyes, nose, lips and chin injured. Third eye on forehead. Hair combed back and arranged in the same fashion as in B44. In front of the head-dress, defaced effigy of a Dhyāni Buddha seated cross-legged. The exact position of the hands of the Dhyāni Buddha cannot be ascertained with accuracy. Late Mediæval.

B49. Head (height 4″) of a (?) female figurine. Reddish grey sandstone. Left ear and nose missing; eyes damaged. Wears necklace and ear-pendants. Hair combed back from forehead, raised and held in by an ornamental band resembling a tiara. Late Mediæval.

B50. Head (height 4″) of a figure of white sandstone. Ear-lobes missing. Wears a peculiar, high head-dress with a trident shaped ornament in front. The figure probably served as the left-hand attendant in a group. Mediæval.

B51. Head (height 5¼″; width 5¼″) of a figure of dark purplish sandstone with part of a halo behind. Ear-lobes broken. Hair combed and arranged in two tiers in the same way as in B42. *Tilaka* mark on the forehead. Late Mediæval.

B52. Head (height 4¼″) of a figure of buff red sandstone with open mouth and protruding lower lip. Hair marked by cross lines. Late Mediæval.

B53. Head (height 2¾″) of dark grey sandstone. Left ear missing. Hair combed and arranged in a chignon behind. Late Mediæval.

B54. Front portion of a small head (height 1¾″) of grey sandstone. Ears missing. Bridge of nose remarkably flat. Late Mediæval.

B55. Statuette in two pieces (height 7¾″) of a female figurine of dark-grey sandstone. Fore-arms and legs below knees missing. Wears necklaces, ear-rings and elaborate head-dress with a stupa in front. Traces of scarf on shoulders. Back slab broken. From Temple 21; 2′ 4″ below surface. Late Mediæval.

B56. Plaque (height 3¾″) of dark green steatite with four-armed Vishnu standing on a cushion wearing ornaments. Tiara mutilated. In his upper hands the god holds a mace in the right and a *padma* in the left. The lower hands rest on the heads of two attendants standing one on either side, the left hand probably holding a *śaṅkha*. Found from the trench, south-east of Building 23, 1′ below surface.

B57. Plaque (height $6\frac{3}{4} \times 3\frac{1}{2}''$) of purplish sandstone with a clumsy imitation of four-armed Vishṇu erect. The deity wears ornaments and a peculiar head-dress possibly derived from the tiara of Indra in the Early School. The hair is hanging on shoulders. In his upper hands the god holds a *gadā* in the right, and a *chakra* in the left; the lower left hand holds a *śaṅkha*, the right raised to the level of the head. To left of Vishṇu, crude figure of seated Gaṇēśa; to right, a standing devotee. The plaque is arched at the top. (Pl. XIX)

B58. Fragment (height $2\frac{3}{4}''$) of a plaque of dark grey sandstone with waist and legs of a Vishṇu (?) figure standing on a cushion. The deity holds a conch-shell in the left hand. To his right, two attendants standing; to left, seated Gaṇēśa and another standing figure. Late Mediæval.

B59. Fragment (height $2\frac{3}{4}''$) of a plaque of buff slate-stone similar to the preceding one. Traces of a crude figure of Gaṇēśa to left and of an attendant to right. Late Mediæval.

B60. Fragment in 2 pieces (height of both pieces $4\frac{3}{4}''$; width $3\frac{3}{4}''$) of a plaque of green slate-stone representing the waist and portion of legs of a (?) Vishṇu figure standing between tapering pilasters. Late Mediæval.

B61. Fragment (height $1\frac{3}{8}''$) of a plaque of buff brown sandstone bearing the head of a Vishnu (?) figure wearing a peculiar head-dress somewhat resembling that of No. B57. Traces of attendants to left. Late Mediæval.

B62. Plaque (height $4\frac{7}{8}'' \times 2\frac{1}{2}''$) of buff slate-stone bearing a clumsy figure of a frowning deity standing on a cushion. Probably four-armed. Wears ornaments and a peculiar winged head-dress. The lower hands are stretched down and rest on uncertain objects; the upper ones hold ends of a long garland, which shows in front of his knees. Found from the Museum site, north trench; 4′ below surface. Late Mediæval.

B63. Fragment (height $3\frac{1}{2}''$; width $4\frac{1}{8}''$) of a plaque of slate-stone bearing the head of a deity. Third eye on forehead. Hair combed and arranged in the same way as in B42. The right hand holds an uncertain object. Small hole to right of the head shows that the plaque was probably hung against a wall. Late Mediæval.

B64. Fragment (height $3\frac{1}{4}''$) of a plaque of dark grey slate-stone bearing the bust of a male figure resembling No. B63. The (? upper) hands are raised and hold ends of the garment. Late Mediæval.

B65. Plaque (height 4″) of black slate-stone bearing a figure of Gaṇēśa with outspread ears seated in the easy posture. Third eye on forehead. Elephant goad in the right hand, vessel of cakes in left. The lower right corner of the plaque is broken. Late Mediæval.

B66. Plaque (height $3\frac{1}{8}''$) of brownish grey slate-stone bearing a seated figure of Gaṇēśa with one tusk and outspread ears. The third eye is marked on the forehead. Hands on knees. Tusk in the right hand, vessel of cakes in left.

B67. Plaque (height $2\frac{1}{8}''$) with a crude imitation of a figure of Gaṇēśa seated. Chocolate coloured sand-stone.

B68. Plaque (height $2\frac{1}{4}''$) similar to B67.

B69. Fragment (height $5'' \times 2\frac{3}{4}''$) of a plaque of white soap-stone representing the waist and legs of *Mahishamardinī*. The back of the buffalo demon is being pierced with a trident. The right foot of the goddess is placed on the demon's head which touches the ground, while with her left hand she has caught the right hind leg of the buffalo and has raised and pressed it backward until the hoof nearly touches the hip.

9

B70. Mutilated figure (height $3\frac{7}{8}'' \times 3\frac{1}{8}''$) of *Mahishamardinī* clad in thick *dhoti*. Buff brown slate-stone. Head, arms and breasts missing. The right foot of the goddess is placed on the back of the demon while with her left hand she holds his lower jaw and pushes it back with such force that the horns touch the back which is also being pierced with a trident. The execution is very clumsy. Late Mediæval.

B71. Mutilated figure in three pieces (height $4\frac{5}{8}'' \times 3\frac{3}{4}''$) of a god seated in the easy posture (*līlāsana*). Buff coloured slate-stone. Head, right arms, left hands and right hip missing. Wears sacred thread and ornaments. The right foot of the diety is placed on a prostrate demon wearing high head-dress and ornaments and holding a sword in his right hand. Crude figure of (?) Gaṇēśa to left and of an attendant to right. From Building 20, 3′ 8″ below surface. Late Mediæval.

B72. Mutilated figure in two pieces (height $4\frac{1}{4}'' \times 2\frac{3}{8}''$) of four-armed female deity standing wearing elaborate *dhoti*, head-dress and ornaments. Black stone. Feet and right upper arm missing. An indistinct object in the left upper hand; lower hands rest on the heads of attendants standing at either side. Late Mediæval.

B73. Fragmentary plaque (height $3\frac{1}{8}'' \times 2\frac{1}{4}''$) of white soap-stone bearing a damaged headless female figure standing. Staff in the right hand; drapery or sword in the left. Crude representation of an attendant standing to right. Late Mediæval.

B74. Fragment (height $3\frac{3}{8}'' \times 2\frac{3}{4}''$) of a plaque of buff red sandstone representing the upper half of a female deity with an attendant standing to left. Bead decoration above and at the sides of the principal figure. About 12th century A.D.

B75. Plaque (height $2\frac{3}{8}'' \times 3''$) of light green steatite representing a female figure with legs wide apart. She has no head or arms, but in place of the head we see a half lotus and in place of arms, heads of *makaras*. Late Mediæval.

B76. Fragment ($1\frac{1}{4}'' \times 1\frac{3}{8}''$) of a plaque of dark-grey steatite representing the waist and legs of a standing figure. Remnants of long garland in front of knees. The feet of the figure are missing. Late Mediæval.

B77. Plaque (height $2\frac{3}{4}''$; width $2\frac{1}{2}''$) of dark-grey slate-stone bearing a clumsy representation of a small bird. Found north of the Museum, 2′ below surface. Late Mediæval.

B78. Plaque (height $3\frac{1}{2}''$; width 2″) of a dark-grey sandstone representing a very rude figure of a four-armed goddess standing, wearing ornaments. The exact nature of the objects held in the four hands cannot be ascertained. Late Mediæval.

B79. Lamp (*chirāgh*)—($8\frac{1}{2}'' \times 4\frac{3}{4}''$) of dark-grey sandstone.

B80. A stopper (height $5\frac{1}{4}''$, thickness at top 3″) of buff-red sandstone. The top resembles an upturned vase in shape; the lower portion is square and tapers downward. Late Mediæval.

B81-89. Nine circular stones of varying dimensions probably used as weighing measures. The sides are somewhat irregular and rough dressed.

Diameters:—$1\frac{7}{8}''$; $2\frac{1}{8}''$; $2\frac{7}{8}''$; $3\frac{1}{8}''$; 3″; $3\frac{3}{4}''$; 4″; $4\frac{1}{8}''$.

Thicknesses:—$\frac{1}{2}''$; $\frac{5}{16}''$; $1\frac{1}{8}''$; $\frac{7}{8}''$; $\frac{1}{2}''$; $\frac{3}{4}''$; $1\frac{1}{4}''$; $\frac{7}{8}''$.

B90-91. Two dabbers ($3'' \times 3\frac{7}{8}''$; $2\frac{3}{8}'' \times 2\frac{3}{8}''$) one of buff-grey and the other of bluish-grey sandstone.

B92-107. Sixteen balls of white or dark-grey sandstone varying from $\frac{1}{2}''$ to $1\frac{3}{8}''$ in diameter some of these are well rounded, others rough and not quite spherical. These might have been used as weights or as balls in cross-bows.

C.—Antiquities in the North Room.

[Nos. C1-815, catalogued by Mr. Ram Chandra Kak.]

Iron Objects.

C1. Spearhead (?) (length $9\frac{5}{8}''$; width of blade $1\frac{1}{8}''$). Double edged-blade; both faces slightly convex; flat spike for insertion into the shaft.

C2. Spearhead (?) (length $6\frac{5}{8}''$; width of blade $1\frac{3}{8}''$), leaf-shaped edge and sharp and well preserved point; round spike partly broken. A longitudinal central ridge produces a certain convexity of the blade. Remarkably fine specimen.

C3. Spearhead (?) (length $7\frac{5}{6}''$; width of blade $\frac{3}{4}''$). Lower end of the blade broader than that of No. C2; one edge nearly straight; round elongated spike.

C4. Spearhead(?) (length 8″; width of blade $\frac{3}{4}''$). Leaf-shaped; both edges damaged. Spike marked off from the blade by a small bead or stop.

C5. Spearhead (?) (length $6\frac{1}{8}''$; width of blade $1\frac{1}{4}''$). Similar to No. C3. Blade damaged. The five specimens described above appear to be too slender to be effective spearheads, yet they are much too large to have been used as arrowheads. The fact, too, of their being provided with thin tangs instead of sockets, would militate against their being spear heads. They may be javelins which could be hurled at an object from a short distance.

C6. Spearhead (length 15″; width of blade 1″). Socketed. The lower half of the blade is four-flanged and the upper half plain, leaf-shaped, and convex on both sides. Flanges deep and sharp. Their grooves run right down to the mouth of the socket. (Pl. XVII)

C7. Spearhead (length $7\frac{5}{8}''$; width of blade 1″). Leaf-shaped; sharp edged blade, convex on both sides; lower end, circular and socketed, and marked off from the blade by a bead or stop. Preservation excellent, except for the edges which are slightly damaged. (Pl. XVI)

C8. Spearhead (length $7\frac{3}{4}''$). Flat blade replaced here by a tapering, sharp pointed spike, square in section; circular socket at lower end.

C9. Spearhead (length $12\frac{3}{8}''$). Somewhat similar to No. C8.

C10. Spearhead (length $13\frac{1}{2}''$). Another socketed specimen in which the usual flat blade has been replaced by a tapering spike, square in section and in this instance barbed at the base. A little above the barbs is a small notch on each edge of spike. The stop below the base consists of three bands or collars; the middle one is broad and flat on the top and bordered by two shallow incised lines. The socketed part is elongated and unusually slender.

C11. Spearhead (length $12\frac{3}{8}''$). Leaf-shaped blade, with sharp, square, spiked point. The base also has been squared and directly surmounts the bead or stop, which is bordered on the lower side below by an elevated latitudinal rib, now almost entirely gone. The mouth of the socket as well as the edges are damaged. It is interesting to note that the sockets in all the examples described above have been formed of flat plates of iron hammered into shape on a conical mandril.

C12. Object (length 6″). It is too decayed to allow of its original shape and use being determined with certainty. It has a sharp tapering tang and the blade appears to have been leaf-shaped. It might have been a lance-head or, what is, perhaps, more likely, a ploughshare of the type described below.

G 2

C13. Dagger. Three fragments only extant. The longest fragment (1′ 5″) comprises the hilt and the expansion of the blade next to it. The hilt is only $2\frac{1}{4}$″ long and is, therefore, much too short for the hand of a grown-up person. It is in a single piece and consists of an elongated ovaltransverse guard and a pommel similar in shape, with a round handle or grip joining the two. The latter is hollow and a spike projecting from the expansion of the blade passes through the transverse guard, handle and pommel, to be rivetted to the outer side of the latter. (Pl. XVII).

C14. Dagger (length $14\frac{7}{8}$″; width of blade $\frac{5}{8}$″). Edges and hilt partly damaged. The latter is $2\frac{1}{4}$″ long and similar in shape to that of No. C13. (Pl. XVII).

C15. Dagger blade (length $5\frac{3}{4}$″). Edges mostly broken off; fragment of the spike projecting from the expansion still extant.

C16-17. Fragments (length $4\frac{3}{4}$″ and 3″ respectively) of the expansions of two daggers. The spike in No. 16 is complete but in the other, only the stump remains.

C18-19. Fragments (length 5″ and $6\frac{7}{8}$″ respectively) of the fore parts of daggers. In No. C19 the point is well preserved. It also has longitudinal ridges on both sides which are discernible only on close inspection.

C20. Barbed arrowhead (length $6\frac{1}{8}$″). Double-edged; spike for insertion into the wooden shaft in perfect preservation.

C21. Barbed arrowhead (length $3\frac{1}{2}$″). Lower end socketed for reception of wooden shaft.

C22. Barbed arrowhead (length $3\frac{1}{8}$″). Similar to No. C21. (Pl. XVI).

C23. Fragment (length $2\frac{5}{8}$″) of the blade of an arrowhead. Leaf-shaped; both sides flat and much corroded.

C24. Arrowhead (length 4″). Double-edged; short spike at the lower end.

C25. Arrowhead (length $3\frac{1}{8}$″). Similar to No. C24. Point missing; spike thick in the middle and tapering towards both ends.

C26. Arrowhead (length $3\frac{5}{8}$″). Spike long and tapering to a point. Much corroded.

C27. Arrowhead (length $5\frac{1}{2}$″). Spike unusually clonated.

C28. Arrowhead (length $3\frac{3}{4}$″). Must have been barbed. Lower end socketed.

C29. Arrowhead (length $7\frac{1}{4}$″). Long narrow, leaf shaped and double-edged blade marked off from the spike by a four-sided stop.

C30. Arrowhead (length $3\frac{3}{8}$″). Trapezoidal blade, flat and sharp-edged. Point damaged.

C31. Arrowhead (length $2\frac{7}{8}$″). Similar to No. C30, but with a thicker blade and bevelled edges. (Pl. XVI).

C32. Arrowhead (length $2\frac{3}{4}$″). Similar to the last, but damaged.

C33. Arrowhead (length $3\frac{5}{8}$″). Bevelled blade with well pronounced central ridges on either face. (Pl. XVI).

C34. Arrowhead (length $2\frac{1}{2}$″). Blade replaced by four sided spike, square in section.

C35. Arrowhead (length $2\frac{7}{8}$″). Similar to No. 33 but with a notch on each face near the spike. (Pl. XVI)

C36. Arrowhead (length $3\frac{3}{8}$″). Similar to No. C34.

C37. Arrowhead (length $2\frac{5}{8}$″). Octagonal point, decorated at the base with a band of two incised lines and marked off from the spike by a circular stop.

C38-39. Arrowheads (length $2\frac{1}{2}$″ and $3\frac{3}{4}$″, respectively) with spiked points

C40. Arrowhead (length $2\frac{3}{4}$″). Similar to No. C34.

Monastic and Household Utensils.

C41 & 41(*a*). Fragments (height 2½″) of two iron-bells. One is semi-oval in shape; the other, furnished with a well preserved ring, has a sharply conical body.

C42. Ring (diameter 8½″) of a tripod; triangular in section. Such tripods appear to have been used as stands for cooking vessels.

C42(*a*). Fragment (diameter 8″) of a similar ring.

C43. Fragment (height 3¾″; diameter 6¼″) of a cooking vessel or *dēgchī*. Rim and bottom missing. The body—a narrow latitudinal band—is attached to the shoulder at the base of the neck. Much corroded.

C44. Nine fragments (length varying from 2½″ to 12″) of a large pan.

C45. Fragment (height 2″; diameter 7″) of a bowl. Bottom and part of rim missing.

C46. Fragmentary hanging lamp (4⅛″ square). The angles have been shaped into wick-holders. Each side has a hole below the rim for passing the wire through.

C47. Fragment (length 7⅞″) of a ladle.

C48. Knife-blade (length 7⅜″; width ¾″). Edge and point broken. Short tapering tang at the lower end. The absence of a rivet hole in the tang shows that the blade could not be folded back into the handle.

C49. Knife-blade (length 7″, width ⅞″). Cutting edge entirely broken.

C50. Knife-blade (length 5⅜″; width ⅞″). The upper edge begins straight but on nearing the further end, is sharply slanted off to the point. The tang has a rivet hole.

C51. Fragment (length 3½″; width ¾″) of a knife-blade similar to No. C50.

C52. Fragment (length 4⅞″; width ⅜″) of a knife. Blade and handle are in one piece. The latter has a pointed end.

C53. Fragment (length 3⅝″; width ½″) of a knife-blade.

C54. Razor (length 7⅝″; width 1 3/16″). The blade is curved and its lower end bent round its own axis so as to form a short round handle.

C55. Razor (length 6″; width 1″). The blade broadens towards the outer end. There is no rivet hole in the tang. (Pl. XVI)

C56. Razor (length 4½″; width 1⅛″). Similar to No. C55.

C57. Razor (length 4½″; width 1⅛″). Rectangular in shape; short thin tang.

C58. Razor (length 4½″; width ⅝″). Slightly curved blade; short thick oblique tang.

C59. Razor (length 3¼″; width ⅜″). Similar to the preceding example.

C60. Sugarcane peeler (height 4⅝″; width 4″). Cutting edge, as usual with modern tools of the same nature, to the inside. Spikes at either end of the blade are joined together and form the tang which was inserted into the wooden haft. (Pl. XVI)

C61. Vegetable cutter (diameter 8⅝″; width of blade 1″). Blade curved inwards; short tang at one end for insertion into the haft, which is usually large and flat. While using the knife it is necessary to keep it firm by placing one foot on the haft. The blade then stands upright with the cutting edge facing the operator who squats on the ground.

C62. Needle (length 5¼″).

C63. Antimony rod (length 5¼″).

C64. Ferrule (length 6¼″). Conical in shape with the vertex downwards. It must have been used for tipping the lower end of a wooden staff or spear.

C64 (*a*). Fragment (length $4\frac{7}{8}''$) of a ferrule. Similar to No. C64.

C65. Stirrup (height $4\frac{3}{8}''$). It has a broad sole which at the ends, is turned vertically upwards and then rounded. Lower part of the aperture which admitted the leather strap is still extant.

Agricultural Implements.

C66. Ploughshare (length $15\frac{5}{8}''$; width $3\frac{1}{2}''$). Broad leaf-shaped blade, flat on one side and convex on the other. Edges blunt. Long tapering tang rectangular in section.

C67. Ploughshare (length 14″; width $2\frac{7}{8}''$). Similar to No. C66. One edge slightly damaged.

C68. Ploughshare (length $13\frac{1}{4}''$; width $3\frac{1}{4}''$). Blade slightly thicker than in the preceding examples. Lower part of the edges straighter and the upper more sharply curved.

C69. Ploughshare (length $10\frac{3}{8}''$; width $3\frac{1}{8}''$). Similar to No.C66 but with the point rounded off.

C70. Ploughshare (length $13\frac{1}{8}''$; width $2\frac{1}{8}''$). It appears to have been originally broader than it is now, but the edges have, on a subsequent repair, been turned upwards, making both the sides flat.

C71. Ploughshare (length $11\frac{7}{8}''$; width 3″). Similar to No. 66. Edges are broken off.

C72. Smoothing ploughshare (length $21\frac{3}{4}''$; width of blade $3\frac{5}{8}''$), locally known as *pāns*. The blade has two vertical tangs, one at each end, which are fixed into the flat wooden back. When the ground has been ploughed and the surface is still loose and uneven, this ploughshare is used to smoothen it. It is worked with bullocks like the ordinary plough. It is also commonly used for removing old stubble from the fields. (Pl. XVII)

C73. Smoothing ploughshare (*pāns*) (length $22\frac{1}{2}''$; width $3\frac{3}{4}''$) similar to No. C72.

C74-77. Tool scrapers (length varying from $3\frac{1}{4}''$ to $4\frac{3}{4}''$). Hollow and chisel-like in shape with edges flat and blunt.

C78-79. Tool scrapers (length $3\frac{3}{8}''$ and $3\frac{1}{16}''$ respectively) similar to the preceding examples.

C80-86. Fragments (diameter varying from $4\frac{1}{2}''$ to $8\frac{1}{4}''$) of sickles.

C87. Fragment (diameter $9\frac{3}{4}''$) of sickle, semi-elliptical in shape. The half near the handle is blunt and round.

C88-89. Fragments (diameter 8″ and $7\frac{1}{2}''$ respectively) of sickles similar to No. C87.

C90. Sickle (diameter $11\frac{3}{4}''$). Semi-circular in shape.

C91-92. Sickles (diameter $9\frac{1}{4}''$ and $9\frac{1}{2}''$ respectively). Similar in shape to No. C90.

C93. Sickle (diameter $10\frac{3}{4}''$). Point broken. The base of the blade is blunt and flat on one side and convex on the other. The top of the tang is adorned with a small barb.

C94. Sickle (length of tang $7\frac{5}{8}''$ and diameter of blade $4\frac{7}{8}''$). It has an unusually long tang with a very slightly curved blade and resembles two arms of a right angle with the angle rounded off.

C95. Sickle (diameter $9\frac{1}{4}''$). Blade resembles the arc of an ellipse. (Pl. XVI)

C96. Sickle (diameter $7\frac{1}{4}''$). Semi-elliptical in shape. The point of the blade is spiked. This feature was probably intended to facilitate the eradication of any extraneous vegetation in the cornfield.

C97. Sickle (diameter $7\frac{1}{4}''$). Similar to No. C96, but without the spiked point.

C98. Sickle (diameter 8″). Similar to No. C87.

Artisans' Tools.

C99-100. Blacksmith's pincers (length 17½" & 14¼" respectively). (Pl. XVII)

C101. Blacksmith's anvil (height 5"). Both top and bottom square. (Pl. XVI)

C102. Blacksmith's hammer (length 7"; thickness 1⅜"). (Pl. XVI)

C103. Garden pick (length 4¾"). Socketed.

C104. Wedge (?) (length 6¼"). It is an unusually massive specimen and has two contiguous depressions on two adjacent sides, the purpose of which is difficult to determine.

C105-111. Wedges (length varies from 1⅞" to 6"). Two of them (Nos. 108-109) were discovered in the mortice of the Gupta column in front of the North Gateway, where the builders had inserted them to keep the column in position.

C112. Fragment (length 6") of a pinchbar.

C113-114. Carpenters' chisels (length 6⅞" and 7" respectively). The upper end is socketed for reception of the haft.

C115-116. Carpenters' gouges (6½" and 5½" respectively). The cutting edge is concave. The upper end is spiked for insertion into the haft. (Pl. XVI)

C117-118. Carpenters' (?) chisels (length 5" each). Upper end solid and square.

C119. Carpenters' chisel (length 8⅛"). Upper end socketed. The socket, as in the case of all such implements described here, is formed by beating out one end of the tool and then hammering it on a conical mandril.

C120. Object (length 4¼"). Chisel-like and socketed. Has a lunate edge. It may be either a carpenters' chisel or what is, perhaps, likely, the ferrule of a staff.

C121-122. Carpenters' awls (length 5" and 6⅝" respectively). Upper ends are hollow for insertion of the wooden handle.

C123. Stone masons' trowel (length 7¼"). It is curved and leaf-shaped. (Pl. XVI)

C124-125. Shoemakers' awls (length 6¾" and 5⅞" respectively). No. C124 has a bulbous body with a long point and spike at the top for insertion into the wooden handle. No. C125 has a flat top. (Pl. XVI)

C126. Awl (length 12"). It has a simple, rounded, and comparatively thick top, and does not appear to have been intended to be fitted with a wooden haft. It can still be used, as it is, without any incovenience.

Household Fittings.

C127. Lock (length 7¾"; height 2¼"; width 1¼"). It comprises two detachable members. The right hand one, in which the key was turned, is box-like in form with three bands on the outside to add to its strength. It has a long horizontal spike at the top which is inserted into the staple of the left hand member. The latter consists of the vertical staple attached to a horizontal plate, the outer end of which has been fashioned into a fan-tail shape. Its inner end is furnished with three projecting tongues, two in a row above, and one below. Each tongue is made up of three pieces disposed one above the other. The middle piece is a little longer than the other two, which are nailed to its further end. When the entire length of the tongues is inserted, through the corresponding apertures, into the hollow right hand member, the free ends—those nearest the holes which admitted them—spring wide apart and effectively prevent the lock from opening. The turning of the key presses the arms of the tongues close together and confines them within the dimensions of the aperture, which results in the members being instantly detached. (Pl. XVIII)

C128. Lock (length $4\frac{1}{2}''$), similar to No. C127. Left hand member missing. There are two bands on each of its longer sides. Keyhole entire.

C129. Fragmentary plate (length $1\frac{5}{8}''$) of a lock. Two of the holes, which were meant for the admission of the tongues, are still entire.

C130. Key (length $7\frac{1}{8}''$). The base is flat with a rectangular opening in the middle. In the middle of the outer edge of each of its longer sides, a chip has been bitten off. Upper part of the handle is flat with a semi-circular top. (Pl. XVIII)

C131. Key (length $6\frac{5}{8}''$). It is fragmentary. The upper part of the handle is flat and has a small hole below its top, probably for passing a string through it.

C132-137. Door chains (length varies from $4\frac{3}{4}''$ to 18″) with and without staples.

C138. Chain (length 23″) of a hanging lamp.

C139-146. Staples (length varies from $1\frac{7}{8}''$ to $9\frac{1}{8}''$).

C147-151. Door rings (length *i.e.*, length of staple *plus* diameter of rings, varies from $4\frac{1}{4}''$ to 6″) with staples.

C152-172. Door (?) rings (diameter varies from $1\frac{1}{8}''$ to $2\frac{1}{2}''$) without staples.

C173. Door ring (length 7″) with staple.

C174. Ring (diameter $1\frac{1}{8}''$).

C175. Ring (length $3\frac{5}{8}''$).

C176. Circular band (diameter 2″, depth $\frac{3}{4}''$). Much corroded. It appears to have been the handle of an iron pan; the rivet hole is still in fair preservation.

C177-187. Clamps (length varies from 4″ to $7\frac{5}{8}''$) with nails. Each comprises a single flat plate with a hole at each end, through which nails are passed. This type of clamps is commonly used in woodwork.

C188-191. Clamps (length varies from $6\frac{1}{2}''$ to $8\frac{1}{4}''$). Each consists of a single piece, rectangular in section with the ends spiked and bent.

C192-195. Clamps (length varies from $5\frac{3}{4}''$ to $14\frac{3}{4}''$). Each of them is a single piece flat and oval in the middle and spiked at both ends. Their general appearance is like that of a stirrup.

C196. Clamp (length 7″). It is a single plate doubled over, with two holes on each of its arms for insertion of nails. The holes on the opposite arms correspond with each other, so that the same nail could be passed through both the holes and then rivetted.

C197. Nail (length 4″) of a clamp similar to No. C196.

C198. Plate (length 7″) with three holes.

C199-200. Fragments (length $3\frac{3}{8}''$ and $2\frac{5}{8}''$ respectively) of plates similar to No. C198.

C201-202(*a*). Circular bosses (diameter of the boss varies from $1\frac{3}{8}''$ to $2\frac{5}{12}''$) with round-headed nails.

C203-220. Round-headed nails (varying in length from 4″ to 2′ $1\frac{3}{4}''$).

C211-228. Nails (length varies from $5\frac{3}{4}''$ to $8\frac{1}{2}''$) with flat triangular heads.

C229-388. Nails (varying in length from $\frac{7}{8}''$ to 9″). The heads are flat and of various shapes. Some have their upper ends merely flattened out and bent to one side only. Others have projecting circular rims, and yet others have projections on two sides only. There are a few which appear to be headless.

C389. Door (?) ornament (length 13"). It resembles in shape a conventional peacock and has holes in the head, body and tail for insertion of nails. It is in a single piece and is quite flat on both sides. (Pl. XVII)

C390-391. Hooks (height $8\frac{5}{8}$" and $7\frac{3}{4}$"). S-shaped. Upper end flattened out and perforated. Lower end, sharp.

C391(*a*). Hook (height $9\frac{3}{4}$"). Similar to the preceding specimens.

C392. Hook (length 6"). Forked. The arms of the fork nearest the juncture are bent over and flattened. The thin end of this flat apex is carried up vertically and bored with one hole for passing through the nail or wire. These hooks could very well have been used as spits.

C393-394. Rods (length 13" each). Thick in the middle and tapering towards each end.

C395-401. Fragments (length varies from 4" to $11\frac{7}{8}$") of rods.

C402. Rod (length $12\frac{7}{8}$"). Similar to Nos. C393 and C394.

C403-405. Rods. (length varies from $2\frac{5}{8}$" to $14\frac{1}{4}$"). Square in section. The ends of No. C403 are bevelled.

C406-408. Rods (length varies from $3\frac{1}{8}$" to $18\frac{1}{4}$"). Rectangular in section.

C409-421. Circular bands (varying in diameter from $\frac{7}{8}$" to $2\frac{1}{4}$" and in depth from $\frac{3}{4}$" to $2\frac{1}{2}$"). They must have been used as holders for wooden or bamboo staffs.

C422-425(*a*). Oval bands (varying in diameter from $2\frac{1}{4}$" to $3\frac{1}{4}$" and in depth from $\frac{1}{2}$" to $\frac{5}{8}$").

C426. Horseshoe-shaped band (diameter $1\frac{3}{4}$" and depth $\frac{3}{4}$").

C427. Fragment (diameter $1\frac{1}{4}$" and depth nearly $1\frac{3}{4}$") of an oblong band.

Miscellaneous and uncertain objects.

C428. Object (length $7\frac{3}{4}$"). It is an ordinary rod with one end flattened out and shaped into a leaf the point of which is bent over. It may possibly be a mud scraper.

C429. Object (length $3\frac{1}{2}$"). It is a thin plate tapering to one end. The broad end is semi-circular and has a sharp edge.

C430. Object (length 4"). Similar to No. C429 except that its sharp edge is slightly bent.

C431. Object (length 5"). It is a rod, hollow at one end and looped at the other. Through the loop is passed a thin ring which may possibly be the link of a chain. The fragment tapers towards the looped end.

C432. Object (length $10\frac{1}{8}$"). It is a rod with one end flattened and spiked perhaps for insertion into a wooden handle. The spiked end is marked off from the body of the rod by two flat lugs.

C433. Object (length $8\frac{1}{2}$"). Similar to No. C432 except that its pointed end is squared instead of being flattened.

C434. Rod (length 11"). Curved at one end.

C435. Object (length $5\frac{1}{4}$"). It is a thin plate broad and perforated at one end and tapering to a point at the other. The point is somewhat curved and the edge appears to have been sharp. It may have been the blade of a knife.

C436. Object (length $3\frac{1}{2}$"). It is a round rod with tapering ends. One of the points is bent over. It appears to be fragmentary.

C437. Object (length $3\frac{1}{2}$"). It is a rod, thin in the middle and thick at the ends which are pointless. It has a disc near one end. A small detachable ring was found on the rod. It may be a spindle whorl.

H

C438. Object (length $4\frac{1}{4}''$). It is a curved plate, with ends rounded off, and a hole in the middle. There is a shallow groove running lengthwise in the middle of one of its faces. It may be the transverse guard of a dagger hilt.

C439. Object (length $2\frac{3}{4}''$). A ring is passed through the loop of a small hook from which hang two fragments of thin plate, evidently forming one complete link. One of these fragments has a disc-shaped body with a narrow neck.

C440. Object (diameter 7″). It is a bent rod with a loop at one end. The closing end of the loop has a disc-shape. The object is fragmentary.

C441. Fragment (diameter $7\frac{1}{4}''$) of an object similar to No. C440 but with a plain looped end.

C442. Object (length $1\frac{3}{4}''$). It is a thin plate. The upper end is fan-like and cusped. It was probably a piece of ornamental furniture.

C443. Object (length 4″). It consists of two rings linked together and a key-like nail hanging from one of them. The larger of the two rings is bent inwards.

C444. Object (length $9\frac{3}{4}''$). It is a rod bent in the middle with two small upright barbs at each side of the angle.

C445. Object (length $4\frac{1}{8}''$). It is a rod with one end bent and flattened. The other end which is also flattened, is triangular in shape with a hole in the middle. It might be part of a stand for wall lamps.

C446-447. Fragments (diameter 4″ and $8\frac{1}{2}''$ respectively), possibly of hooks. Each has a flat end with a hole in the middle, which in one example is broken.

C448. Two fragments (diameter $2\frac{1}{8}''$ and length $3\frac{1}{2}''$ respectively) of rods with one end pointed. One of them is curved.

C449. Fragment (length $4\frac{1}{2}''$) of a rod. At one end it has two broken spikes projecting at right angles to it.

C450-451. Fragments (diameter $6\frac{1}{2}''$ and $4\frac{3}{8}''$) of two curved rods.

C452. Fragment (length 3″) of the link of a chain. It has been twisted several times over.

C453. Fragment (length $2\frac{7}{8}''$) of a thick plate bent at one end and with a large hole at the other.

C454. Object (length $5\frac{7}{8}''$). A flat fragmentary blade with a tang. It may have been used as a garden tool.

C455. Object (length $8\frac{1}{4}''$). It appears to be a knife with a long narrow leaf-shaped blade, and a short handle which is now bent.

C456. Object (length $3\frac{1}{12}''$). It has a blunt triangular blade from the apex of which projects a long pointed spike. Its purpose is uncertain.

C457-462. Fragments (length varying from 2″ to $7\frac{1}{3}''$) of plates with and without holes for nails.

Bronze Objects.

C463. Bowl (diameter $7\frac{3}{4}''$; height $2\frac{3}{8}''$). Straight plain rim. Bottom flat and partially broken. Turned on the lathe. (Pl. XIX)

C464. Bowl (diameter $3\frac{3}{8}''$; height $1\frac{1}{8}''$). Thick straight rim, ornamented both inside and outside with grooved lines. Bottom missing. Turned on the lathe and highly polished.

C465. Bangle (diameter $2\frac{5}{8}''$). Oval in shape. Thick at the back and tapering towards both ends. It is ornamented with rows of dots arranged in geometrical patterns. The ends

—one of which is slightly damaged—have a longitudinal slit, both arms of which are perforated. It appears that there was a detachable member which could be dovetailed into the slit and made fast with a pin. (Pl. XVI)

C466. Bangle (external diameter $2\frac{3}{8}''$). Circular in shape. Comprises two members both of which are round, solid and plain. The ends of the larger member have a slit, both arms of which are perforated, as in No. C465. The smaller member is dovetailed into these slits but the pins, which held it fast, have disappeared. (Pl. XVI)

C467. Bracelet (diameter $1\frac{3}{4}''$). Circular in shape. Thin plate. Outer face convex and inner concave. The former is decorated with shallow spirals and clusters of small incised circles. Much of this decoration is now defaced.

C468. Fragment (diameter $1\frac{5}{8}''$) of a plain bracelet similar in shape as No. C467.

C469. Bracelet (diameter $2\frac{1}{4}''$). Inner face flat and outer convex. Ends soldered with each other.

C470. Finger ring (diameter $\frac{5}{8}''$). Plain and thin.

C471. Finger ring (diameter $\frac{3}{4}''$). Made of plain round wire. Resembles a betel leaf with the broad end bent inwards. When the ring is worn the broad bent side faces the palm and the pointed end nearly touches the knuckle.

C472. Fragment (diameter 1″) of an ornamental ear ring.

C473-475. Rings (diameter varies from $1\frac{1}{8}''$ to $1\frac{3}{8}''$).

C476. Pendant (height $\frac{7}{10}''$) of an ear ornament. It has an approximately cylindrical body with a rounded top which is surmounted by a small point. It has an ornamental rim projecting below.

C477. Figurine (height $3\frac{3}{4}''$) of a four-armed goddess standing on a pedestal under an arched canopy which is supported on two pillars with capitals and bases. The arch is surmounted at the extremities by thin ornamental peaks. The two upraised hands of the goddess hold a sword and a pitcher and the other two are hanging down, apparently empty, by her sides. She is clad in a short *dhoti*, with an elaborately ornamental hem. The loose end of the *dhoti* dangles between her legs. She wears a conical crown, ear ornaments, necklaces reaching down to her breasts and bangles. Late mediæval epoch. (Pl. XVIII)

C478. Bell (height $2\frac{1}{4}''$). Conical body with round rim at the base and a circular fillet a little more than half-way up the vertex. The top of the bell is perforated, and surmounted by a vertical loop round which is twined a piece of flat copper wire. It is from a fold of this wire, which is thrust through the hole at the top, into the body of the bell, that the tongue hangs. The latter is a plain piece of metal with a hook at the top.

C479. Rod (1′ $12\frac{3}{4}''$). Thick in the middle and tapering towards the ends.

C480. Object (length $6\frac{5}{8}''$). It is a long narrow plate with a barb at one end and a hole in the middle. At the other end is a flat S-shaped projection, with a cusped lower edge.

Copper Objects.

C481. Cooking vessel (*degchī*) (height $5\frac{5}{8}''$; diameter at top $4\frac{1}{2}''$). The bottom is hemispherical in shape, and the body conical, with the top truncated. The rim springs straight from the shoulders and has a groove on the upper face along the edge. (Pl. XVIII)

C482. Bell (height $4\frac{3}{8}''$). It is composed of two pieces; the lower one of which is nearly cylindrical. The upper is rounded like a cap and soldered on to the former. Tongue missing.

H 2

C183. Bell (height $3\frac{7}{8}''$) with tongue. It has a large, flat and partly damaged ring at the top. The tongue is suspended from a hooked nail which passes out through the top of the bell and is rivetted with the ring. (Pl. XVI)

C184. Bell (height $2\frac{1}{4}''$). The ring on the top is passed through a hole and rivetted inside. Tongue missing.

C185. Miniature bell (height $\frac{7}{8}''$). It has two holes, one at the top and another just above the lower rim, the purpose of which is not clear.

C186. Bangle (diameter $2\frac{1}{4}''$). It is a plain copper rod bent into a circular shape.

C187. Finger ring (diameter $\frac{7}{8}''$) with crystal gem. (Pl. XVI)

C187(*a*). Fragments (diameter $\frac{7}{8}''$) of a ring.

C188. Ear cleaner (length $3\frac{3}{4}''$). It is a thin straight rod with a punched bead decoration in the middle. The ends are flattened and bent. (Pl. XVI)

C189. Antimony rod (length $4\frac{7}{8}''$). Thin in the middle and thick at the ends. (Pl. XVII)

C190. Eight fragments (diameter ranging from $1\frac{1}{2}''$ to $4\frac{1}{4}''$) of bowls and saucers.

C191. Fragment (diameter $2\frac{1}{8}''$) of a tin ring, possibly a bangle.

C192. Zinc bangle (diameter $1\frac{5}{8}''$).

Early Glazed Pottery..

(About 3rd Century B.C.—1st Century A.D.)

C193. Neck (height $2\frac{1}{4}''$; diameter of mouth 3″) of water vessel. The rim which projects downwards is decorated with four grooved lines running parallel to the outer edge of the mouth. Red colour wash and glaze.

C194. Neck (height $2\frac{5}{8}''$; diameter of the mouth 3″) of a water vessel. Its plainness is relieved by two round mouldings, one at the base and another up in the middle. The rim is rounded off and everted. This fragment possesses a special human interest inasmuch as the finger prints of the potter who joined the neck with the body of the vessel still exist in all their original freshness, after a lapse of two thousand years and more.

C195-496. Fragments (diameter $5\frac{3}{8}''$ and 5″ respectively) of water vessels, probably *surāhīs*. Both of them have round mouldings at the base of the neck.

C197. Neck (height $2\frac{5}{8}''$; diameter of mouth $2\frac{1}{2}''$) of water vessel. It is cuplike in shape. The outer face is divided into three horizontal sections which are separated from each other by round latitudinal ribs. The rim is straight. Red colour wash and glaze.

C198. Neck (height. $4\frac{3}{8}''$; diameter of mouth $2\frac{3}{8}''$) of a *surāhī*. The rim radiates outwards and is quadrantal in section. The lip projects upwards, and the neck proper tapers both ways towards the middle. (Pl. XX).

C199. Neck (height $4\frac{1}{8}''$) of *surāhī*. Similar to No. C498 but with a cup-shaped mouth and rim. The lower edge of the neck is carefully ground and must have been joined to the body of the vessel with some kind of glue.

C500-505. Necks (height ranging from $2\frac{3}{4}''$ to $4\frac{3}{4}''$). Similar to No. C499. The original coat of red colour wash still survives on most of them. (Pl. XX).

C506-522. Necks (height ranging from $1\frac{3}{4}''$ to $5\frac{3}{8}''$) of *surāhīs*. The most remarkable feature of this type is the rim, which though flat, convex, or cuplike in different specimens is invariably surmounted by a tapering nipple which in some cases is plain and in others ornamented with round mouldings. The neck tapers both ways towards the middle except in one instance where it is nearly cylindrical. The red colour wash and glaze are quite fresh and bright on the better burnt specimens. (Pl. XX)

C523-525. Nipples (length varies from $\frac{3}{4}''$ to $1\frac{3}{4}''$) of *surāhīs*, with moulded rims.

C526-539. Spouts (length varies from 1″ to $3\frac{7}{8}''$) of water vessels. They have circular rims and pointed bottoms. They were made separately and attached to the vessel before baking. The corresponding space on the vessel, instead of having one single hole, is perforated like a sieve, which has the advantage of preventing straw or insects from getting in, without obstructing the passage of water. The original coat of red colour wash still exists on the majority of them. No. C530 is covered with a thick coat of brick dust which appears to have extended all over the original vessel, perhaps with the purpose of lessening, to some extent, the effects of sudden changes of atmosphere on its contents. It has a projecting rim. The back of No. C531 has been neatly ground, probably, after the vessel to which it belonged was broken.

C540. Potters' dabber (diameter $1\frac{1}{2}''$). Made of fine reddish clay, and glazed. (Pl. XX)

C541. Spindlewhorl (diameter $1\frac{1}{2}''$). Lower face concave and upper convex. A hole in the middle. Dark red colour wash with glaze.

C542-544. Potsherds (length ranging from $1\frac{1}{8}''$ to $2\frac{3}{8}''$). Grey clay with black glaze. No. C544 possesses some remnants of a coat of black slip.

C545-548. Potsherds (diameter varying from 3″ to $5\frac{1}{4}''$). Dark buff colour wash and glaze.

C549-566. Potsherds (diameter ranging from $1\frac{5}{8}''$ to $5\frac{1}{2}''$). Red slip with glaze. The shades of colour wash vary from dark red to light red. Most of these sherds appear to have belonged to water vessels.

Miscellaneous Pottery of the Gupta and the Mediæval periods.

C567. *Hāndī* (height $2\frac{1}{4}''$; diameter $2\frac{3}{4}''$). Flat bottom. Short everted rim. A grooved line round the body. Buff coloured clay, indifferently baked. (Pl. XXI)

C568. *Hāndī* (height $3\frac{7}{8}''$; diameter at top $3\frac{3}{4}''$). Spherical bottom. Body of the vessel ornamented with groups of grooved lines. Rim short and projecting outwards. Dull black colour all over the body except the rim which is partially dull red. Coarse clay, underburnt. (Pl. XIX)

C569. Top (height $1\frac{1}{2}''$; diameter 3″) of water vessel. Mouth, narrow with broad radiating rim. The shoulder which springs from the body of the vessel is concave. Red clay, underburnt. Traces of red colour wash.

C570. Top (height $2\frac{1}{4}''$; diameter $3\frac{1}{4}''$) of water vessel. Everted rim. Base of the neck decorated with narrow plain band in low relief. Shoulders concave as in No. C569.

C571. Top (height $14\frac{3}{8}''$; diameter at top $22\frac{1}{4}''$) of a vessel. Thick, slightly convex and projecting rim. Immediately below the rim are two cable mouldings from the lower one of which is suspended another cable arranged in swags of irregular dimensions. The body is nearly cylindrical. Coarse buff clay with a coat of red slip.

C572. Water vessel (height 8″; diameter of mouth $4\frac{1}{8}''$). Globular body with a short plain spout projecting a little above the middle. A plain moulding runs round the neck. The rim is vertical with a concave outer face. Coarse red clay. Traces of red slip. (Pl. XVIII)

C573. Water vessel (height $3\frac{1}{4}''$; diameter of mouth 2″). Similar to No. C572 but with a plain neck and rim.

C574. Fragment (height $5\frac{3}{8}''$) of a water vessel. Short spout. Plain, tall and narrow neck.

C575. Jug (height $3\frac{7}{8}''$). Drum-like body, broad in the middle and narrowing towards the ends. Rim plain and upright. Coarse reddish clay. (Pl. XXI)

C576. Jug (height 3"). Flat base. Two grooved lines round the body a little below the middle. (Pl. XXI)

C577-579. Vessels (height ranging from $1\frac{1}{2}''$ to $2\frac{1}{4}''$). No. C577 has a spherical body and short upright neck; No. C578, flat base and a grooved line round the middle of the body and No. C579, a flat base and a nearly oval body. The neck of the last is broken. (Pl. XXI)

C580. Saucer (diameter $3\frac{3}{4}''$). Flat bottom, steep everted sides. Inner side has traces of a coat of powdered mica and sand. Light red colour wash mixed with a sprinkling of mica. This treatment gives the saucer a polished and sparkling surface. (Pl. XXI)

C581-589. Lids (height ranging from $2\frac{3}{8}''$ to $5\frac{1}{2}''$). They are shaped like solid plugs tapering downwards and surmounted by umbrella-like caps. The latter is crowned by a flat-topped boss which might, very well, have served as a handle. Red clay, with traces of red colour wash and in some cases of red slip. (Pl. XIX)

C590. Lid (diameter $4\frac{7}{8}''$). Sides slope to the bottom where they meet. A grooved line on the upper surface midway between the rim and the bottom. A short cylinder in the centre to serve as a handle. Coarse red clay mixed with mica.

C591-592. Lids (diameter $3\frac{5}{8}''$and $4\frac{7}{8}''$ respectively). Saucer-like in shape. No. C591 has a boss in the middle to serve as a handle. In No. C592 the boss is cylindrical with a concave top. Coarse red clay. (Pl. XIX)

C593. Lid (height $3\frac{3}{4}''$; diameter at base $7\frac{3}{8}''$). Nearly hemispherical in shape with a short "axehead" handle. Hollow inside. Outer surface bears four vertical streaks of red colour which mark off the quadrants.

C594. Stopper (?) (height $1\frac{7}{8}''$). Resembles a square nail with semi-circular boss and the nail head projecting above. Lower part curved. It is fragmentary and made of fine red clay.

C595-597. Stoppers (height varying from 1" to $2\frac{1}{4}''$). Flat topped. Rough coarse clay badly baked and uncoloured.

C598. Nipple (height $1\frac{1}{2}''$) of the spout of a water vessel. Conical in shape. Base decorated with a row of dentils.

C599-600. Spouts (length $1\frac{3}{4}''$ and $1\frac{1}{8}''$ respectively) of water vessels. Mouth surmounted by two mouldings behind which rises a gable ornament. The head of the gable as well as the ends of the mouldings ornamented with rings. A plain triangular projection below. A fourth ring ornament marks the lowermost extremity of the juncture of the spout and the vessel. (Pl. XX)

C601-611. Cups (height varies from $1\frac{5}{8}''$ to $2\frac{5}{8}''$ and diameter from $3\frac{1}{4}''$ to 5"). Sides radiate upwards to the rim which is plain and slightly convex. Bottom flat. Coarse red clay, badly burnt. (Pl. XXI)

C612. Lamp (length $4\frac{5}{8}''$). Circular body with sides sloping inwards and ornamental fantail projection behind. Long spout with deep groove for the wick. Flat bottom. Traces of black paint and (?) glaze. (Pl. XXI)

C613-617. Lamps (diameter varies from $1\frac{3}{8}''$ to $2\frac{3}{4}''$). Shallow, saucer-like shape. Short flat base. This type of lamp is generally used for illuminations on festive occasions, such as the *dīpāvali* (*divāli*). (Pl. XXI)

C618. Lamp (?) ($3\frac{1}{2}''$). Rectangular, trough-like shape. A short handle on one of the shorter sides. On the opposite side are traces of what might have been a spout. Red clay with traces of colour wash. (Pl. XXI)

C619. Inkpot (height $1\frac{7}{8}''$). Square. Ornamented with two raised bands, one round the shoulder and the other round the base. Upper edge of the top band is free and forms a groove round the circular neck. Traces of red paint, and, over that, of a coat of lime slip still exist. (Pl. XXI)

C620-623. Fragments (diameter varying from $4\frac{1}{4}''$ to $5\frac{3}{4}''$) of *hāndīs*. Buff clay with a considerable sprinkling of mica, which gives these fragments a sparkling surface. The mixture of mica has the additional advantage of making the ware very durable.

C624. Potsherd (diameter $6\frac{1}{2}''$). It is very thick and must have belonged to a large vessel. Coarse red clay. Decorated with a band of double leaf ornament. Remnants of a coat of red slip.

C625-626. Potsherds (diameter $7\frac{1}{4}''$ and $7\frac{3}{4}''$ respectively). They are fragments of the rim of a large vessel. The lip is rounded off. Below it is a peculiar decoration which appears to have been formed by pressing an ordinary round moulding, while it was wet, between the thumb and the forefinger, producing, as it now is, a double row of circular depressions, on an applied fillet. Coarse clay, underburnt.

C627. Potsherd (diameter $4\frac{3}{4}''$). Decorated with mouldings and a row of ornamental depressions similar to that of Nos. C624-625 except that in this instance the row is single instead of being double. Coarse buff clay.

C628. Bossed potsherd (length $3''$). Light red clay with traces of lime wash.

C629. Potsherd (diameter $3\frac{1}{8}''$) possibly belonging to a *surāhī* or water vessel. Decorated with two bands of ornaments, the lower one consisting of a row of rosettes and the upper one of small round bosses. These rows are separated from each other by circular fillets. Dark grey clay, coated with black paint, which is now faded.

C630. Potsherd (length $2\frac{5}{8}''$) ornamented with vertical rows of double lines in relief, which are transversely intersected by numerous small incisions in the intervening flutes.

C631-633. Potsherds (length varying from $2\frac{7}{8}''$ to $3\frac{3}{8}''$). Coated with red slip, and decorated with streaks of black paint which must have run round the body of the vessel. Coarse clay.

C634. Potsherd (length $2\frac{3}{4}''$). Covered with red slip. A broad band of the original surface has been left uncoated and is of a smooth buff colour.

C635-637. Potsherds (length varying from $1\frac{5}{8}''$ to $4''$). Ornamented with rows of small incisions. Red colour wash. Coarse buff clay, underburnt.

C638-640. Potsherds (length varies from $1\frac{1}{2}''$ to $3\frac{5}{8}''$). Ornamented with closely set vertical chain mouldings.

C641. Potsherd (length $2\frac{1}{8}''$). Ornamented with conventional palm-tree decoration. Red clay with colour wash.

C642. Potsherd (diameter $1\frac{3}{4}''$). Appears to have belonged to the rim of a bowl. Pale reddish slip. It has curious dark spots on both surfaces.

C643. Potsherd (diameter $5\frac{1}{2}''$) belonging to the rim of a *hāndī*. Buff clay with pale reddish slip, similar to that of No. C642.

C644. Flesh scraper or strigil (length $3\frac{5}{8}''$). Has rows of irregular oval and rectangular depressions on both sides. The original surface has worn off. Coarse reddish clay with red colour wash. (Pl. XX)

C645. Fragment (length $2\frac{7}{8}''$) of flesh scraper or strigil. It has a number of incised lines on each side intersecting one another at right angles, thus forming a tolerably rough surface. Red clay.

C646-647. Spindle whorls (diameter 2″ each). Rim curved upwards. Lower face concave. Dark grey clay with black slip on the upper face.

C648-649. Spindle whorls (diameter $1\frac{3}{4}''$ and $1\frac{7}{8}''$ respectively). Conical in shape with the top truncated. Coarse clay, underburnt. No. C649 appears to have been washed in red colour.

C650. Spindle whorl (diameter $1\frac{5}{8}''$). Conical in shape. Cone begins from a short cylindrical base. Coarse clay, underburnt.

C651. Finial (height 8″). Hollow, conical in shape with a slightly rounded base. Decorated with bands of incised lines. A small hole in the middle seems to be accidental. Coarse black clay, badly burnt. Traces of black paint.

C652. Finial (height $3\frac{7}{8}''$). Hollow; conical in shape. Top broken. Red clay, well burnt. Traces of red slip.

C653. Finial (height $5\frac{1}{4}''$). Conical in shape with slightly bulging sides. Base is fragmentary and is decorated with two plain convex mouldings. Coarse clay with red slip on the upper surface.

C654. Fragment (height $2\frac{1}{8}''$) of a (?) finial. Upper part conical and separated by a ledge from the lower which is concave. Coarse clay with red colour wash.

C655. Fragment (diameter $2\frac{1}{8}''$) of an ornamental wheel or disc. Upper surface flat and ornamented with spokes or rays radiating from the centre and encircled by two rings, the outer one of which has a denticulated border. The lower surface is convex and has a hole in the centre which, however, does not penetrate through. It is made of red clay, with red colour wash. (Pl. XXI)

C656. Fragment (length $1\frac{3}{8}''$) of an ornamental leaf. Red clay and traces of red slip.

C657. Fragment (length $1\frac{3}{8}''$) of an object resembling a reel. The cylindrical neck is perforated. One outer face is adorned with a rosette, the other which is fragmentary seems to have had a lotus pattern incised upon it. The object may be an ear ornament. Red clay with red colour wash and slip.

C658. Object (diameter $1\frac{1}{8}''$). It is a reel of dark coloured clay and was perhaps used as an ear ornament.

C659. Object (height $\frac{1}{2}''$). Nearly cylindrical in shape with slightly concave sides. The upper surface is decorated with a spiral of incised dots within an irregular circle.

C660. Object (length $1\frac{5}{8}''$). It is cruciform in shape with one arm slightly longer than the other. It might have been used for twining thread upon.

C661. Clay object (length $3\frac{1}{8}''$), resembling the head and trunk of an elephant but with the features left unindicated. The clay is unburnt or if burnt at all, it must have been very slightly exposed to fire. Traces of greyish slip and over that, of lime wash.

C662. Bead (length $2\frac{1}{8}''$) of burnt clay coated with sand. Oval in shape and perforated lengthwise. The coat of sand was probably applied to afford a strong backing to the original surface which has now disappeared. The bead might also have been used as a net-sinker.

C663-703. Beads (diameter varying from $\frac{3}{4}''$ to $1\frac{1}{2}''$) of clay, burnt or only sundried. They are hemispherical in shape, with the top truncated. There is a groove round the hole both at the top and the base. They are buff, black or reddish in colour.

C704. Roof tile (length $9\frac{5}{8}''$; width $6\frac{1}{2}''$). Flat on both sides. Two holes below the upper edge for insertion of the pins. The lower end, which is thicker than the upper one, is flat on one side and convex on the other. Coarse reddish clay, burnt.

Terracottas.

C705. Fragment (height $3\frac{7}{8}''$) of the *ushnīsha* of a large Buddha figure. Many of the spiral curls are in good preservation. It was originally coated with lime slip, abundant remnants of which still exist. The core is composed of coarse red clay mixed with sand and small river *bajri* which baking has transformed into one compact mass. (Pl. XIX)

C706-736. Votive *ushnīshas* (height ranging from $\frac{1}{4}''$ to $1\frac{3}{4}''$). They are simple spiral cones in shape, and their colour varies from red to dark buff. They are made of somewhat coarse clay, indifferently burnt. Few of them show any traces of colour wash. (Pl. XIX)

C737. Fragment (height $6\frac{7}{8}''$) of an upper arm and elbow of a human figure. The upper arm is draped upto the elbow which is bare. Remnants of a thick coat of lime slip still exist.

C738. Fragment (length $2\frac{3}{8}''$) consisting of two broken fingers of a large figure. Traces of at least two coats of lime slip may still be perceived.

C739-740. Fragments (length $2\frac{1}{4}''$ and $1\frac{1}{2}''$ respectively) of two fingers. A hole running lengthwise through each of them, indicates that they were pinned to the hand to which they belonged. Traces of yellow slip with lime wash over it.

C741-742. Fragments (height $3\frac{1}{4}''$ and $1\frac{7}{8}''$ respectively) of hair. No. C741 is a coil of hair tied with a double cable-like plait. Hairs are indicated by curved incised lines. It bears a thick coat of coarse lime wash over an original coat of slip which had partly peeled off. There are also traces of rosy paint and glaze. No. C742 consists of the upper part of the coil. Its core is made of river *bajri* mixed with clay. Traces of red paint with a thick coat of lime slip, which is still in tolerably good condition.

C743. Fragment (length $1\frac{3}{4}''$) of a curl of hair. Dull red clay.

C744. Object (height $2\frac{7}{8}''$). It resembles the torso of a human figure on a circular pedestal. In place of the arms there are clumsy heads of two conventional animals. On the breast and back are two holes, which correspond with each other though they do not run through. The purpose of this curious object is uncertain. Remnants of red paint exist all over the body. (Pl. XIX)

C745-749. Fragments (height ranging from $2''$ to $3\frac{3}{8}''$) of the heads of (?) conventional elephants. The temples and the protuberance on the forehead are particularly prominent. The latter resembles a circular boss. A thick rib runs round it and projects downwards, perhaps, to indicate the outline of the trunk. All these fragments have pin-holes running vertically between the temples and through the trunk. They are covered with a coat of lime slip which has in many places cracked and peeled off.

C750. Object (length $3\frac{3}{8}''$) resembling the trunk of an elephant decorated with two bands of ornaments. Bears traces of a coat of red slip.

I

C751. Conventional animal (height 3″). Legs damaged. Beak-like head surmounted by two small protuberances which may possibly be the ears. Mane indicated by shallow transverse incisions on the nape of the neck. Body slopes downwards from the neck towards the rump. Short stumpy tail. Traces of red colour. (Pl. XIX)

Terracotta Plaques.

C752-808. Fragments (height varying from $\frac{5}{8}$″ to 6″). The original plaque was broad and leafshaped with a scalloped border. It had a plain pedestal below and was surmounted by a circular seal with a pointed top on which was stamped the sacred Buddhist creed :—*Yē dharmāḥ hētuprabhavāḥ*, etc. The central panel of the plaque bore in bold relief the figure of the Buddha, seated on a lotus throne, with his left hand in his lap, palm upwards, and his right touching the ground, symbolical of the moment when " he called upon the earth to bear witness to his right to remain where he was and the earth replied with so mighty a voice that the armies of Mara fled discomfited." He has an oval halo round his head, with long-stalked lotus buds waving on either side of it. In the corners a little above his shoulders are two small relic caskets surmounted by three umbrellas with streamers flying. Underneath these and filling the vacant space between them and the knees of the Buddha is repeated the sacred creed over again. Still lower, opposite to his knees is a lotus bud with a long stalk projecting from the foundations of the throne. The palæographical characteristics of the letters and the discovery of the plaques themselves under the pavement of Temple 18 fix their date between the 6th and 7th centuries of the Christian era. Light red slip is still discernible on many of the fragments. (Pl. XVIII)

C809. Fragment (height 1$\frac{7}{8}$″) of a deeply recessed plaque with a slightly scalloped outer border. The Buddha is seated on the lotus throne in the gift-bestowing attitude (*vara-mudrā*). In the vacant spaces, on either side of him, is stamped the sacred creed. The characters are similar to those of the preceding examples. Buff coloured clay with reddish paint.

C810. Fragment (height 1$\frac{1}{2}$″) of a plaque. The head of the Buddha figured here has a remarkably prominent nose, sloping forehead, a broad mouth and a receding chin. That it is the head of the Buddha is evident from the presence of the *ushnīsha*. Reddish clay.

C811. Fragment (height 1$\frac{5}{8}$″) of a plaque. The fragmentary figure of the Buddha is seated on a throne in a pillared niche, the plinth of which is ornamented with a dentil course.

C812. Fragment (height 2$\frac{3}{8}$″) of a plaque bearing the bust of a female with elaborate coiffure and ear ornaments.

C813. Cast (diameter 2″) of a circular seal. Bears three relic caskets arranged in a row on the top, and the saceed Buddhist creed stamped below. It is made of red clay and is fragmentary.

C814. Cast (diameter $\frac{7}{8}$″) of a seal probably bearing the impression of the Buddhist creed. Letters are quite indistinct.

C815. Cast (diameter 1″) of a seal bearing the impression of the Buddhist creed in six lines within a circle. From the forms of the letters it appears that this cast is probably later in date than those described above.

C816. Broken oval die (length 2$\frac{1}{4}$″ ; width 1$\frac{3}{4}$″) of light green steatite. The engraving is divided into two sections by a horizontal band of zig-zag lines. The upper section contains a wheel flanked by lotuses above and 2 antelopes with long horns seated face to face below. The lower section contains remnants of floral designs and monograms. The lower and right sides of the tablet are broken.

Found E. of Tope between group of stupas.

C817. Amulet shaped die (height $\frac{7}{8}''$; width $1\frac{1}{8}'' \times \frac{1}{2}''$) of greyish green steatite with a monogram. Hole in the top for thread.

C818. Lower portion (height $1\frac{3}{8}''$; out diameter $2\frac{7}{8}''$) of a relic-casket red steatite in 2 pieces. Turned on lathe and decorated with delicately defined bands on the body. ? Gupta.

C819. Lid (diameter $2\frac{5}{8}''$; height $1\frac{1}{8}''$) of a casket of buff red steatite in two pieces. Turned on lathe.

C820. Another lid (diameter $1\frac{5}{8}''$) of a small casket. Rim damaged. Purplish grey soapstone.

C821. Spindle whorl (diameter $2\frac{1}{8}''$) of pinkish grey steatite with 2 holes in the centre.

C822. A cylindrical piece of highly polished red jasper probably used as ear button. Length 1″; diameter 1″.

C823. A similar fragmentary ear button of jasper $1\frac{7}{8}'' \times 1''$.

C824. A reel shaped piece $1\frac{5}{8}'' \times \frac{7}{8}''$ of highly polished black jasper probably used as an ear button.

C825. A pin (length 2″) of black bone or horn with pointed ends. Northward trench, From Museum site. 2′ below surface.

C826. A piece of ivory bangle. Length $1\frac{1}{16}'' \times 1\frac{5}{8}''$.

C827. A piece of glass bangle. $1\frac{1}{16}''$ long.

C828. An oblong bead of blue glass. $\frac{3}{16}''$ long.

C829. Another glass bead. $\frac{5}{16}''$ long.

C830. A round bead of white stone. $\frac{3}{8}''$ height.

C831. A round crystal bead. $\frac{1}{2}''$ height.

C832. A broken ivory dice, ($1\frac{7}{16}'' \times \frac{9}{16}''$) decorated with 3 concentric circles on one side, 2 on top and bottom of the other, and one in the centre of the third. The fourth side has chipped off.

C833. Fourteen fragments of a slab of dark purplish sandstone bearing a Sanskrit inscription in verse in highly ornamental acute-angled *Siddhamatrika* characters of the seventh or eighth century A.D. The greater portion of the slab seems to have been lost and it is not possible to form a correct estimate of the dimension of the inscribed surface or to reconstruct the text. The inscription opened with invocation of Lokanātha and Vajrapāṇi. Then followed a *prasasti* of the kings of Mahamalava, of whom only one name, Sri-Vappakadeva, is found in full and a part only of a second. Sri-Maharaja Sarjasa. Sriparvvata is named in a fragment, and a chief named Rudra, evidently the donor is mentioned in another (=*seshumahasavda sri-Rudra-namadheyenasmi* (*n*).) Found at the site of monastery No. 19.

Coins.

Forty-one coins of the Western Kshatrapas found in 1916-17 in a small earthen vessel about 100 feet to the south-west of the Museum, 1' 6" below surface. They are all of base silver.

Serial No.	Size.	Obverse.	Reverse.	Reference.	REMARKS.
			Rudrasena I.		
C834	·6	Bust of King rt.	Faint traces of *Chaitya*; border of dots. Legend in Brāhmī characters :— *Kshatrapasa Rudrasa[na]*.	Rapson's Cat. of the coins of the Western Kshatrapas, etc., Pl. XII, No. 335.	
			Rudrasena II.		
C835	·55	Do.	*Chaitya* of three arches surmounted by crescent; beneath, waved line; l., crescent; r., star. Legend in Brāhmī characters :— *Rājñaḥ Kshatrapasa Viradāmaputrasa Rājño Mahākshatrapasa Rudrasenasa.*	Rapson Op. Cit. Pl. XV, No. 581.	
C836	·6	Bust of King rt., traces of Greek legend.	Similar to above, but no star to rt. of *Chaitya*:— *Rājñaḥ Kshatra[pa] [rañа] Mahākshatrapasa Rudrasenasa.*	Do.	
C837	·6	Do.	Similar to C835, with border of dots :— *Rājñaḥ Khsatra(pa) .... rājñaḥ Mahakshatrapasa Rudrasanasa.*	Do	
C838	·6	Bust of King rt.	Similar to C835 :— *Rājñaḥ Kshatra[pasa] Varadāmaputrasa Rājño Mahākshatrapasa.*	Do.	
C839	·55	Do.	Similar to C835 :— *Rājñaḥ........ [Vi]radāmaputrasa Rājño Mahākshatrapasa Rudra.*	Do.	
C840	·6	Do.	*Chaitya* of three arches; beneath, waved line; border of dots. Inscription in Brāhmī characters :— *Rājñaḥ Kshatrapasa Viradamaputrasa Rājño (Mahā)-[k]sha[t]ra.*	Do.	

Serial No.	Size.	Obverse.	Reverse.	Reference.	REMARKS.
C841	·55	Bust of King rt.	*Chaitya* of three arches; beneath, waved line; r., star. Legend in Brāhmī characters :— *Rājñaḥ Kshatrapasa V[ī]ra-dāmaputrasa Rā[jño]...... sa Rudrasahasa.*	Rapson Op. Cit., Pl. XV; No. 666.	"ha" is a mistake for "na."
			Viśvasiṃha.		
C842	·6	Do.	Similar to C837 :— *Rājño Ma[hā][k]sha[t]rapasa Viśva[s]ihasa.*	Do. Pl. XV, No. 627.	
C843	·55	Do.	Similar to above, but without waved line beneath the *Chaitya* :— *Rājña Mahāchhatrapa....... sahatvasahana...... [trapasa] Viśvasiṃha.*	Do.	The date is possibly 197.
			Bhartṛidaman.		
C844	·6	Do.	*Chaitya* of three arches, surmounted by crescent; beneath, waved line. Legend in Brāhmī characters :— *Rājño Mahākshatra[pa] ..... naputrasa Rājñaḥ Kshatrapasa Bhartṛidāmnaḥ.*	Do. Pl. XV, No. 666.	
C845	·55	Do.	Similar to C835 :— *Rājño Mahākshatrapasa Rudrasenaputrasa Rājñaḥ. Kshatrapasa Bhartṛi*	Do.	The coin contains the date 19[9]. There can be no doubt about the decimal figure. But only the lower part of the unit figure has remained and shows to be 9 in all likelihood. This is the earliest date known for Bhartṛidāman as Kshatrapa.
C846	·6	Do.	Similar to C835 :— .... *[Rājña] Rudrasenaputrasa Rājña Mahākshatrapasa [Bha](t) [ri]*	Do.	
C847	·6	Do.	Similar to C835 :— .... *Rājña Mahākshatrapasa Bhartṛidāmanah.*	Do	The date is possibly 211.

Serial No.	Size.	Obverse.	Reverse.	Reference.	REMARKS.
C848	·55	Bust of King rt.	Faint traces of *Chaitya*; beneath, waved line. Legend in Brāhmī characters :— .... *Rudrasenaputrasa Rājña Mahākshatra*	Rapson Op. Cit., Pl. XV, No. 666.	
C849	55	Bust of King rt., date, =220.	*Chaitya* of three arches, surmounted by crescent; l., crescent; r., star. Legend in Brāhmī characters :— *Rājño Mahākshatrapa Rudrasenaputrasa Rājñaḥ Mahākshatrapasa Bhartṛidāmnah.*	Do.	The decimal figure in the date looks like 20 and there may be a unit figure too.
C850	·55	Do.	Similar to C835 :— *Rājño Mahākshatrapasa Rudra* .... *Kshatrapasa Bhartṛidāmānaḥ.*	Do	
C851	·55	Bust of King rt.	Similar to C844, but with the waved line beneath the *Chaitya* :— *Rājño Mahākshatrapasa Rudrasena*............*pasa Bhartṛidāmnaḥ.*	Do.	
C852	·6	Do.	Similar to C835 :— ....*Kshatrapasa Rudra[sena]putra [rājño].*	Do.	
C853	·55	Do	Similar to C835 :— *Rājño Mahākshatrapasa Rudrasenaputra*	Do.	
C854	·55	Do.	Similar to C840 :— *Kshatrapasa Rudrasenaputrasa.*	Do.	
			Viśvasena.		
C855	·55	Do.	Faint traces of *Chaitya*; beneath, wavy line; border of dots. Legend in Brāhmī characters :— *Rājño*................ *putrasa Rājño Kshatrapasa Viśvasenasa.*	Rapson's Op. Cit., Pl. XVI, No. 719.	
C856	·55	Do.	Similar to C848 :— ....*tṛidāmputrasa Rājño Kshatrapasa Viśvasenasa.*	Do.	

Serial No.	Size.	Obverse.	Reverse.	Reference.	REMARKS.
C857	·55	Bust of King rt.	Similar to C835 :— *Rājño Mahākshatrapasa Bhatṛi Rājño Kshatrapasa Visvasenasa.*	Rapson Op. Cit., Pl. XVI, No. 719.	
C858	·55	Do.	Similar to C844 :— .... *Kshatrapasa Bhatridāmaputrasa Rājño*	Do.	
C859	·6	Do.	Similar to C835 but without crescent to left of the *Chaitya* :— .... *Bhatṛidāmaputrasa Rājño* .... *Vi.*	Do.	
C860	55	Do.	Faint traces of *Chaitya.* Legend in Brāhmī characters :— *Rājño Mahākshatrapasa* .... *Visvasenasa.*	Do.	
C861	·55	Do.	Similar to C835 :— *Rājño Mahākshatra* .... *Visvasenasa.*	Do.	
C862	·55	Do.	Similar to C835 :— ....*putrasa Rājño Mahākshatrapasa Visvasenasa.*	Do.	
			Rudrasiṃha II.		
C863	·55	Bust of King rt., date, η-[υ] =2[3...]	Similar to C835 :— *Svāmi-Jīvadāmaputrasa Rājño Kshatrapasa Rudrasihasa.*	Op. Cit., No. 774.	
C864	·55	Bust of King rt., traces of Greek legend; date, η-υ[...]= 23[...]	Similar to C843:— *Svāmi-Jīvadāmaputrasa Rājño Kshatrapasa Rudrasihasa.*	Do.	
			Rudrasena III.		
C865	·55	Bust of King rt., date, η-γ[=]=27[2].	Similar to C837 :— ....*Rudradāmputrasa Rājña*....*Mahākshatrapasa Svāmi*	Rapson Op. Cit., Pl. No. 812.	

Serial No.	Size.	Obverse.	Reverse.	Reference.	REMARKS.
			Doubtful or Unidentified Coins.		
C866	·55	Bust of King rt.	Similar to C837 :— .... *putrasa Rājño Kshatrapasa Viśva*........	...	As *sena* cannot be read, the name may be Viśvasena or Viśvasiṁha.
C867	·55	Do.	Similar to C835 but without crescent above the *Chaitya* :— *Rājño Mahākshatrapasa Dāmasenaputrasa Rājño Mahākshatrapasa* (*Vi* ?).	Rapson Op. Cit., Pl. XIV, No. 407.	The King might be Vijayasena(?).
C868	·55	Do.	Similar to C859 :— *Rājño Mahākshatrapa Rudrasahaputrasa Rājño*........	Rapson, Op. Cit., No. 335.	The legend does not give the name of the King nor the date. It only speaks of a son of Rudrasiṁha. The latter had three sons. It is therefore difficult to say to which son the coin belongs.
C869	·6	Do.	Similar to C841 :— .... *Rājño Mahākshatrapasa Rudrasa* [ha-p]u[t] ra........sa.	Do.	Do.
C870	·55	Do.	Similar to C854 :— .... *Kshatrapasa Rudrasa*	Rapson Op. Cit. Pl. XII, No. 335.	
C871	·55	Do.	Similar to C860 :— .... *Manaputrasa Rājña Kshatrapasa.*	Do.	Do.
C872	·55	Do.	Similar to C848 :— ....*Kshatrapasa.*	Do.	Do.
C873	·55	Do.	Similar to C837, but with no star to rt. of *Chaitya* :— ....*putrasa Rājño Mahākshatrapa*	Do.	Do.
C874	·6	Do.	Similar to C837 :— ....*putrasa Rājño Mahākshatra*..............	Do.	Do.

D. Inventory of Sculptures and Minor antiquities in the godown or lying about the site.

In the Godown.

D1. Fragment of Asoka Column ($7'' \times 6''$).

From Gateways of Stupa I.

D2. Fragment ($2' \times 1'$ $6''$) from the E. Jamb of South Gateway. Lotus decoration on the outer face, bust of female on the inner.
D3—17. Small fragments from the jambs of gateways carved with railing patterns and floral or other designs.
D18—20. Three fragments from the same bracket as A 24. Delicately carved with foliage
D21. Fragment from the same bracket as A 25.
D22. Fragment from the leg of a large *Yakshi.*
D23—24. Fragment from the forearms of *Yakshis* wearing bangles.
D25—27. Bunches of mangoes from the brackets.
D28. Fragment of a bracket with left foot of a small *Yakshi.*
D29. Fragment of a bracket with right foot of a small *Yakshi.*
D30. Right foot of a small *Yakshi* wearing heavy anklets.
D31—32. Damaged fragments, similar to D29.
D33. Hand of a small *Yakshi.*
D34—35. Fragments from the forearms of small *Yakshis* wearing bangles.
D36—40. 5 fragments of small brackets carved with mango leaves.
D41—43. Bunches of lotus-buds.
D44—49. 6 fragments from the short uprights separating the architraves. Decorated with lotuses or palmettes.
D50. Bust of a double faced rider. *Cf.* A51.
D51. Right arm of a figure holding drapery in palm.
D52. Fragment carved with forearms of a figure wearing necklace and bangles.
D53. Fragment carved with railing on sides. From a false capital.
D54. Fragment carved with bust of a standing denotee.
D55—57. 3 fragments carved with balustrade patterns.
D58. Mutilated winged lion.
D59—62. Winged lions, fragmentary.
D63—65. Heads of lions, badly damaged.
D66—68. Wings of lions.
D69. Leg of a lion.
D70—71. Pedestals of lions.
D72. Mutilated elephant, large.
D73. ,, ,, small.
D74. Trunk of a small elephant.
D75. Leg of a small elephant.
D76. Fragment of pedestal of a small elephant.
D77—78. 2 fragments of pedestals of large elephants.
D79—94. Fragments from the tridents surmounting the gateways.
D95. Head of a *chaurī* bearer, mutilated.
D96. Hand of a *chaurī* bearer.
D97—98. Tops of *chaurīs.*
D99. Fragment of a wheel (*chakra*).

From the Gateway of Stupa III.

D100—102. Three fragments of wheel (thickness $2\frac{1}{2}''$).
D103. Hips and hind legs of a lion (Ht. $9''$).
D104. Pedestal ($10\frac{1}{2}'' \times 6\frac{3}{4}''$) with claws of a lion (mark the 5 fully developed claws).

F

From the Berm Railing of Stupa II.

D105—111. Fragmentary pillars decorated with lotuses. D109 bears a peculiar design in the central medallion. D111 is inscribed.

D112—140. Fragments of similar pillars. Nos. 112-116 are inscribed.

From the Berm and Ground Railings of Stupa III.

D141—144. Fragments of pillars from the stairway railing.

D145. Fragment of an inscribed pillar from the berm railing.

D146. Broken inscribed cross bar from the ground railing.

Other Early Sculptures.

D147. Fragment of upright similar to A61 and A62 decorated with lotus and palmette designs.

D148. Similar fragment. Full lotus in centre surrounded by 4 *mandipada* symbols alternating with geese in pairs.

D149—150. 2 fragments of similar uprights.

D151—152. 2 fragments (Ht. 7½") from the legs of female figures wearing heavy anklets.

D153. Similar fragment from the leg of a smaller figure.

D154—155. 2 fragments carved with mangoes in relief.

D156. Fragment carved with foliage.

D157. Fragment carved with lotus and balustrade pattern.

D158. Head of a figure in relief, damaged.

159. Torso of a standing figure in relief.

160. Fragment of railing pillar. Lotus design enclosed by bead and reel decoration.

D161. Fragment of railing pillar carved with bust of a figure.

D162. Similar fragment carved with mangoes.

D163. Hips of a figure in the round.

D164. Fragment probably from the same coping stone as No. 125.

D165. Fragment of octagonal pillar decorated with lotus design.

D166. Fragment of a similar pillar.

D167—174. Fragments of pillars from the berm railing or Stupa I (D167 carved with a horse in the central medallion).

D175—198. Broken pavement slabs, bearing Brahmi inscriptions.

D199—201. Inscribed fragments of 3 octagonal pillars from Temple 40.

D202. Pillar from the stairway railing of a Stupa.

D203. Section of a small umbrella relieved with concentric bands and radiating ribs.

D204—214. Fragments of umbrellas with radiating ribs on underside.

D215. Damaged hips of *Yaksha* figure. Similar to Nos. 30 and 31.

D216. Octagonal pedestal with feet of a standing figure.

D217. Bell capital probably from the column to north of Stupa II. A row of large lotus leaves falls on the shoulder of the reeded bell; above which is a cable necking. Tenon at top.

Fragmentary sculptures of the Gupta and late Mediæval periods.

D218. Capital of a pilaster similar to No. A94.

D219. Capital of a pilaster similar to No. A 94, fragmentary.

D220. Bust of a *Yaksha* from similar capital.

D221. Fragment of capital decorated with double lions and plants. *Cf.* Capitals in the porch of Temple 17.

D222. Double lion similar to No. A104.

D223—225. Smaller lions similar to above.

D226—227. Two damaged lions.

D228. Fragment of a lion.

D229. Pedestal and feet of a standing figure.

D230—232. Fragments from the arms of figures. Mathurā stone.

D233. Left hand of a deity. Wheel on palm. Mathurā stone.

Fragmentary sculptures of the Gupta and late Mediæval periods—contd

D234. Right hand of Buddha(?). Wheel on palm. Web between thumb and fore-finger Mathurā stone.
D235. Mutilated hand. Mathurā stone.
D236. Right hand of a Buddha figure.
D237. Fragmentary bust of Buddha preaching.
D238—241. Fragments of halos.
D242. Pedestal with feet of a figure.
D243. Pedestal with feet of a figure (in two pieces).
D244. Headless image of Buddha in Meditation.
D245. Legs of Buddha, standing.
D246. Torso of Buddha standing in the *Abhayamudrā.*
D247. Pedestal and legs of Buddha. Deer and wheel on pedestal.
D248. Headless image of Buddha seated cross-legged and preaching the First Sermon at Sārnāth. On pedestal, wheel flanked by a deer to either side.
D249. Pedestal and legs of Buddha seated in the *bhūmisparsamudrā.*
D250. Mutilated figure of Buddha in the *bhūmisparsamudrā.*
D251—253. Pedestals and legs of 3 Buddha figures.
D254. Legs of a Bodhisattva (?) figure.
D255. Bodhisattva figure broken into 8 pieces which cannot be fitted. Elaborately ornamente 10th-11th Century A.D.
D256. Damaged torso of a goddess standing. Rosary in right hand.
D257. Damaged headless figure of a goddess seated in the *lilāsana.*
D258. Chest and right arms of a four armed goddess. Rosary in upper right arm.
D259. Similar damaged figure.
D260. Fragmentary chest and left arm of a figure.
D261. Damaged figure seated in the *lilāsana.*
D262—265. Lower portions of 4 similar sculptures.
D266. Ganeśa.
D267. *Mahishamardinī*, broken.
D268. Pedestal and feet of a deity standing on lotus. *Preta* squatting to proper right.
D269. *Preta* from a similar sculpture.
D270. Elongated lotus bud from a similar sculpture, with remnants of a Nāgari Inscription.
D271. Elongated lotus bud with right hand of deity and bust of attendant.
D272. Pedestal and right foot of a figure. Elephant on pedestal.
D273. Legs of a standing figure wearing long garland.
D274. Torso of pot-bellied male figure (Jambhāla ?) in the round. Wears necklace and scarf. Uncertain object in left armpit.
D275. Torso of a male figure wearing ornaments.
D276. Torso of a female figure holding *chaurī* in left hand.
D277—278. Busts of 2 female figures.
D279. Mutilated figure of Buddha seated cross-legged on lotus throne.
D280. Buddha head, damaged.
D281. Buddha head, front portion.
D282. Buddha head, small.
D283. Head of a (?) Bodhisattva figure in relief. Miniature stupa to right of the head; lotus buds to left.
D284—286. Heads of 3 figures.
D287. Broken head of a figure.
D288—290. 3 unfinished heads.
D291. Right arm of a figure, fragment of.
D292—293. Right hands of figures.
D294—295. Right hands of Buddha. Wheel on palm.
D296—299. Left hands of female figures.
D300. Chest and right arm of a figure.
D301. Chest of a *Yaksha* figure. Cobra round the neck.
D302. Chest of a *Yaksha* figure (smaller).
D303. Waist and legs of a female figure.

Fragmentary sculptures of the Gupta and late Mediæval periods—contd.

D301—306. Waist and legs of 3 female figures.
D307. Hips and thighs of a figure.
D308. Thighs of a figure. Elaborately ornamented.
D309. Waist of a figure.
D310. Right leg of a figure.
D311. Fragment in 2 pieces of a stele with two vertical compartments. Male figure in the upper compartment with cobra twisted round his right leg and biting the thumb of the left hand; male and female in the lower, the male holding a staff. Part of Buddhist creed on the plain border separating the two compartments. *Cf.* B. 30.
D312. Fragment of stele with damaged female figure seated cross-legged on lotus throne.
D313. Fragment of stele with a standing female figure, holding sword in the right hand resting on the hip.
D314. Fragment of stele with a kneeling devotee.
D315. Large head of a Buddha figure (about 1′×1′).
D316. Fragment from the pedestal and crossed legs of a figure seated on a throne resting on 2 lions, Mathurā stone.
D317—321. Fragments of 5 halos.
D322—325. Halos with gandharvas.
D326—330. Gandharvas.
D331. Top portion of a relief. Damaged Buddha and Bodhisattva figures in the middle. Gandharvas to right.
D332—333. Fragments of sculptures with figures of attendants.
D334. Miniature stupa from the top portion of a relief.
D335. Fragment from the side of a halo. Legs of a figure riding on a curious bridled animal with human legs and horse's neck.
D336. Fragment of sculpture. *Makara* head to left; lion's paw to right.
D337. Lion from a relief. Legs missing.
D338. (?) Base of a rectangular pillar. The lower portion resembles a boat in shape. The sides are moulded.
D339. Fragment of a pilaster in 3 pieces. Damaged *Yaksha* supporting forefront of kneeling elephant in the upper compartment.
D340. Damaged sculpture with forefront of a kneeling elephant.
D341. Head of a demoniac *Yaksha*, damaged.
D342. Fragment of pilaster with lion's head.
D343. Lion's head from a similar fragment.
D344. End portion of a bracket.
D345—346. Two similar fragments.
D347. Fragment of bracket with head of a figure on the under-side.
D348. Sculptured stone elaborately ornamented with arched roof of a shrine relieved with niches.
D349. *Amalaka* with ribs.
D350. Boss decorated with spiral lines.
D351. Boss decorated with a lotus flower.
D352. Capital of a pilaster decorated with foliage on three sides.
D353. Curry stone, semi-circular at top.
D354. Curry stone, fragment of.
D355. Fragment of a slab bearing what might be the plan of a building (?).
D356. Hand-mill.
D357—365. Fragments of slabs with fragmentary Nāgari inscriptions. Dimensions vary from 5½″×3½″ to 1′×1′.
D366. Inscribed fragment from the pedestal of a figure.
D367. Similar inscribed fragment with lion's paw.
D368. Inscribed fragment from a sculpture.
D369. Inscribed fragment of a votive Stupa with Buddha seated in meditation in a niche.
D370—371. Two dabbers.
D372—384. Pestles. Length varying from 1¾″ to 4½″.
D385—418. 34 stone-weights. Flat and roughly circular in shape. Sides, rough dressed. Diameters vary from 1½″ to 5″.

Fragmentary sculptures of the Gupta and late Mediæval periods—concld.

D419—420. Two flat and circular potsherds. Diameter 1½″ and ⅞″ respectively.
D421—428. Six fragments of stone plaques.
D429. Octagonal base of a pillar, circular mortice at top resembling a pivot.
D430. Top portion of a pillar with a Nāgari inscription.
D431. Relief. Śiva seated on a throne supported by his bull. Upper left arm lost; trident with cobra at top in right. Lower left hand holds a vase; right disposed in the *abhyamudrā*. Female attendants on either side.
D432. Pedestal and legs of a figure of Śiva seated in the *lilāsana* on a throne supported by his bull. On his left thigh, Pārvati seated in the *lilāsana*, her left foot resting on the back of a lion. Between the bull and the lion, a kneeling *Yaksha*. To right of Śiva, Ganeśa, with attendant standing behind.
D433. Votive Stupa decorated with 4 niches containing Buddha figures in various attitudes.
D434—438. 5 bricks (11″×11″×2½″) from débris of Stupa I.
D439—440. 2 bricks 14½″×9″×3″ and 13½″×8″×3″.
D441. Bust of a female figure in relief.
D442. Pedestal and feet of a figure standing on lotus.
D443—444. Pedestals (with feet) of 2 figures.
D445. Left foot of a figure.
D446. Right foot of a figure.

Sculptures lying on the site.

Near Stupa III (I) Ground railing of Stupa 3.

D447—460. Broken pillars (D454, inscribed).
D461—494. Smaller pieces of pillars.
D495. Cross bar.
D496—501. Broken cross bars, inscribed.

(II) Berm railing of Stupa 3.

D502—598. Fragments of pillars. (Nos. D502, D503 and D585, inscribed.)
D599—637. Cross bars.
D638—640. Kerb stones.
D641—672. Coping stones.
D673. Kerb stone from the stairway railing of Stupa 3.
D674—675. Fragments of pillars from the *hti* railing of Stupa 3.

Around and about Stupa I.

(i) Ground railing of Stupa I.

D676—738. Broken pillars.
D739—765. Fragments of cross bars.
D766—781. Coping stones (D780, inscribed).

(ii) Berm railing of Stupa I.

D782. Newel post from the Stairway railing.
D783—802. Fragments of pillars from Stairway railing.
D803—849. „ „ „ the berm railing.
D850—859. Cross bars from the berm railing.
D859—877. Coping stones „ „ „

Around and about Stupa I—*contd.*

(iii) Hti railing of Stupa I.

D878—883.	Fragments of pillars.
D884—907.	Broken fragments of cross bars.
D908.	Lid of relic-box from Stupa I (in 5 pieces).
D909.	Large umbrella (broken into many pieces) relieved with radiating ribs on underside.
D910.	Similar umbrella in 3 pieces. Probably from Stupa I.
D911.	„ „ in 2 pieces (smaller) „ „ „

(iv) Miscellaneous.

D912—914.	Cross bars (3′×1′ 6″).
D915.	Broken shaft of Aśōka Column, in 11 pieces.
D916.	Capital of the Śunga Column No. 25.
D918.	Lion capital of Pillar 34.
D919.	Capital of Gupta Column 26.
D920—923.	4 *Dhyāni* Buddhas in the *pardakshina* of Stupa I.
D924.	Image of Buddha in front of Stupa 5.
D925.	Image of Buddha in Temple 31.
D926.	Nāgī figure in front of Temple 31.
D927—945.	Fragments of large octagonal pillars from Temple 40.
D1046—1058.	„ „ small „ „ „ „
D1059—1089.	„ „ octagonal pillars (D959, unfinished; and Nos. D960 and D961 inscribed).
D1090—1096.	Fragments of square pillars.
D1097.	Corner pillar from a solid balustrade.
D1098—1099.	Square uprights „ „
D1100.	Pillar from a solid balustrade, square below and octagonal above.
D1101.	Pillar (Gupta).
D1102.	Fragment of a pillar with inscription of the late mediæval period.
D1103—1116.	Fragments of pillars (Mediæval).
D1117.	Unfinished pillar in 2 pieces.
D1118.	Pilaster (Mediæval).
D1119—1122.	Threshold stones, carved.
D1123.	Capital of a pillar.
D1124—1168.	Bases of pillars, fragmentary.
D1168—1172.	Pedestals of statues.
D1173—1176.	Stone mortar (in 2 pieces).
D1177—1194.	Fragments of hand mills.
D1195—1237.	Plain face stones from a building.
D1238.	Broken umbrella from Stupa 3.
D1239—1269.	Fragments of umbrellas.
D1270.	Fragment carved with a lion and an elephant on lotuses.
D1271—1332.	Votive Stupas.
D1333—1350.	„ „ fragmentary.
D1351—1372.	„ „ (miniature).
D1373—1411.	„ „ top portions of.

Near Temple 18.

D1412.	Corner pillar from Temple 18.
D1413—1414.	Pillars from Temple 18.
D1415—1416.	Capitals of pillars from Temple 18.
D1417—1418.	Lintel stones from Temple 18.
D1419.	Pilaster.
D1420.	Door jamb of Temple 18 (in 2 pieces).
D1421.	Relic box (?) in Temple 18.
D1422—1423.	Slabs from the roof of Temple 18.
D1424.	Similar roofing slab.
D1425—1427.	Fragments of pillars.
D1428.	Base of a pillar.

West of Monastery 47.

D1429. Fragment of square capital with *yakshas* at corners and plant in centre. Early Gupta. (*Cf*. A96 & D232).
D1430. Broken octagonal pillar or umbrella-shaft perforated with a hole through the middle
D1431—1432. Square pillars, unfinished.
D1433. Octagonal pillar, square at base.
D1434—1437. Pillars.
D1438—1443. Fragments of pillars.
D1444. Cup-shaped capital of a pillar.
D1445. Bell-shaped „ „
D1446—1456. Capitals of pillars.
D1457—1458. „ „ „ unfinished.
D1459—1466. Bases of pillars.
D1467. Pilaster relieved with a figure standing in a niche.
D1468. Pilaster carved with a human figure.
D1469—1470. Architectural stones (window frames ?).
D1471—1474. Face-stones.
D1475—1476. Door lintels.
D1477. Door jamb.
D1478. Pedestal and legs of Buddha in the *abhayamudrā*.
D1479—1481. Lower halves of seated figures of Buddha.
D1482. Fragmentary bust of Buddha.
D1483. Seated figure, badly damaged.
D1484. „ „ with attendant, damaged.
D1485—1486. Damaged Kuveras (lower halves only).
D1487—1497. Fragments of sculptures.
D1498—1499. Pieces of halos.
D1500. Pedestal with feet of a figure.
D1501—1510. Pedestals of images.
D1511—1513. Heads of lions, fragmentary.
D1514. Votive stupa with a thousand miniature stūpas on the body.
D1515. Votive stupa with 4 Buddha figures, seated in niches.
D1516—1517. Pedestals of votive stupas.
D1518. Carved stone from a building.
D1519—1520. Frieze stones.
D1521. Pillar from Temple 45.
D1522—1539. Carved face-stones from the *Śikhara* of Temple 45.
D1540. Carved stone decorated with diamond designs.
D1541. Part of a finial.
D1542. *Āmalaka* in 5 pieces.
D1543. Base of *āmalaka* in 3 pieces.

Inside Monastery 47.

D1544—1548. Fragments of railing pillars.
D1549—1554. Fragments from a berm railing.
D1555. Umbrella (in 2 pieces).
D1556—1564. Octagonal pillars.
D1565—1578. Fragmentary pillars.
D1579. Broken pilaster decorated with 2 standing figures.
D1583—1593. Square bases of pillars.
D1594—1610. Capitals of pillars.
D1611—1628. Lintels.
D1629—1637. Face-stones from a building.
D1638. Large circular stone (base of a pillar ?) with a hole in the middle; the surface converges towards the centre.
D1639—1655. Carved fragments.
D1656—1685. Architectural fragments.

Inside Monastery 47—*contd.*

D1686—1687. Curry stones.
D1688—1703. Fragments of a bell-shaped capital.
D1704. Torso of a small standing figure.
D1705—1706. Seated figures, damaged.
D1707. Left half of the bust of a figure.
D1709. Right leg and hips of a seated figure.
D1710. Pedestal and legs of a standing figure.
D1711. Left foot and right leg of a seated figure.
D1712. Pedestal with left foot of a figure.
D1713—1787. Fragments from the arms of figures.
D1788—1803. Legs of figures.
D1804—1805. Knees of figures.
D1806. Fragment with toes of the right foot of an image.
D1807—1862. Fragments of sculptures.
D1862—1874. Fragments bearing remnants of drapery.
D1875—1881. Pedestals of images.
D1882—1902. Fragments of pillars from the berm railing of Stupa 2.

North of Temple 45.

D1903—2191. Carved face-stones from the *Sikhara* of Temple 45.
D2192—2211. „ „ „ „ „ (small fragments).
D2212—2213. Fragments from the *āmalaka*.

South-West of Temple 45.

D2214—2622. Carved face-stones from the *Sikhara* of Temple 45.
D2623—2718. „ „ „ „ „ „ (smaller and broken fragments).

Inside Temple 45.

D2719. Image of Buddha placed against the E. wall.
D2720. Pedestal of an image.
D2721—2723. Fragments of sculptures.
D2724. Door lintel.

In the cells south of Temple 45.

D2725. Buddha in the *bhūmisparsamudrā*.
D2726—2727. Seated Buddhas, damaged.
D2728. Damaged figure.
D2729. Lower half of a figure seated on a chair (damaged).
D2730. Bust of an image.
D2731. Elbow of a figure.
D2732. Broken pedestal with right foot of a figure.
D2733. Fragmentary heels.
D2734. Carved stone.
D2735—2737. Roof slabs.

Near Stupa 2.

(i) *Ground railing of Stupa 2.*

D2738. Corner pillar.
D2739—2741. Fragments of pillars decorated with lotuses.
D2742—2747. Cross-bars.

(ii) Berm railing of Stupa 2.

D2748—2752.	Kerb stones, fragments of.
D2753—2764.	Pillars, ,,
D2765—2845.	Cross bars.
D2846—2887.	,, ,, fragments of.
D2888—2889.	Coping stones ,, ,,
D2890—2891.	Fragments of pillars from the stairway railing.
D2892.	Piece of a corner pillar from the stairway landing.
D2893—2912.	Cross bars from the stairway railing.
D2913—2922.	,, ,, ,, ,, (fragments).

(iii) Miscellaneous.

D2923—2924. Small cross-bars belonging to the berm or *hti* railing of a small stupa.

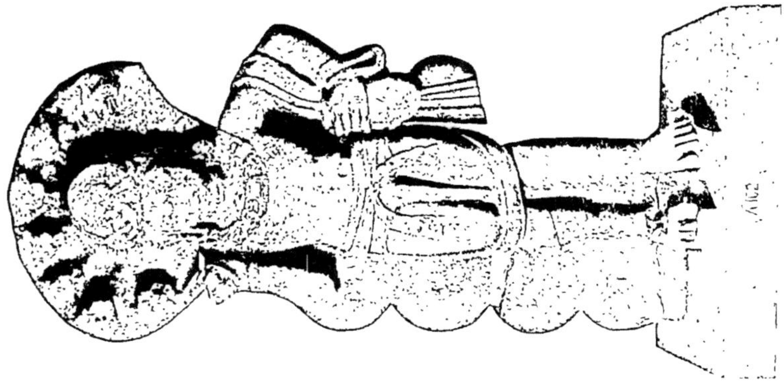

A 102

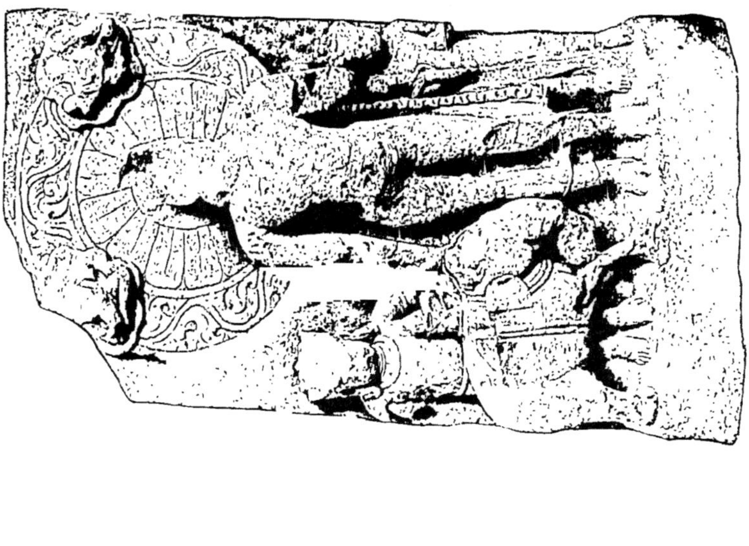

9

19

A 82

23

Photo-engraved & printed at the Offices of the Survey of India, Calcutta, 1921

167

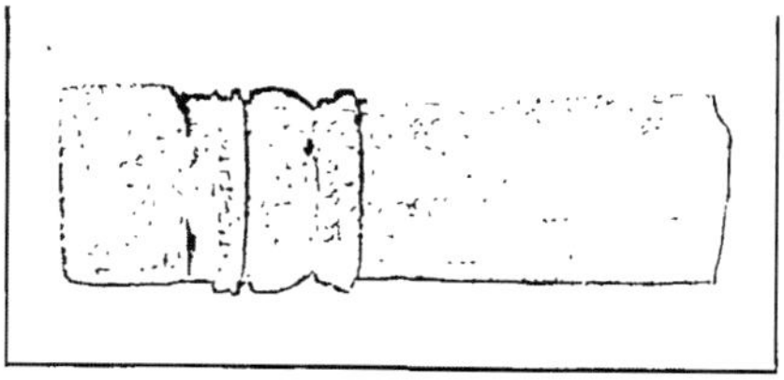

137

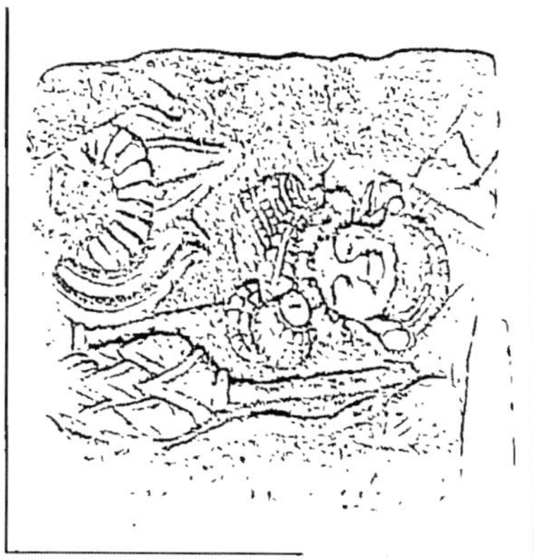

A 70

15

A 1.

A 10.

A 71.

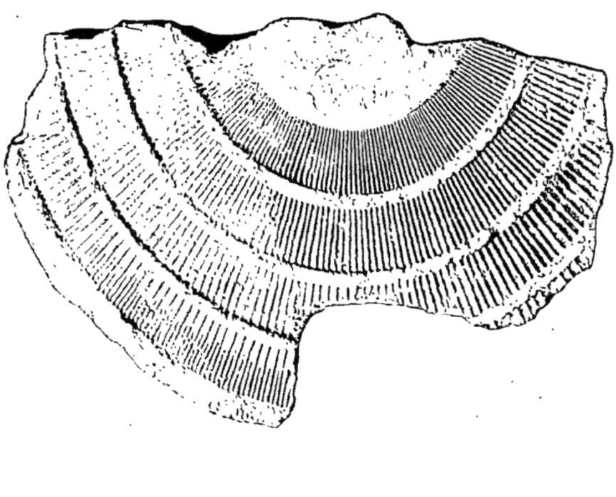

A 2.

A 15

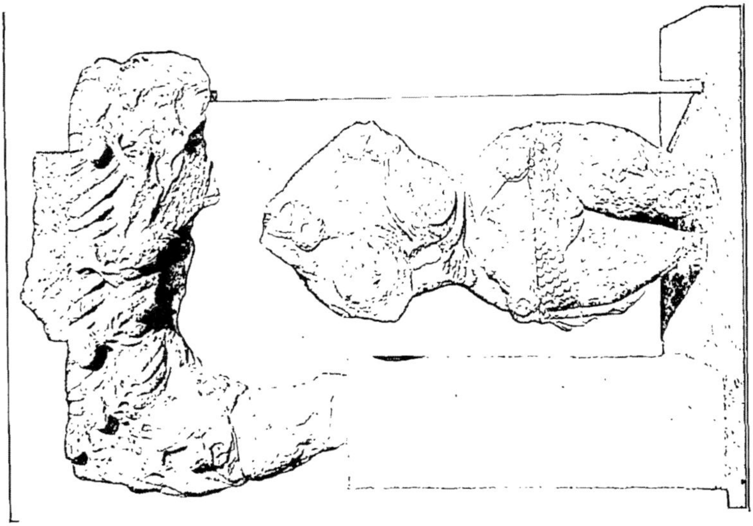

A 28

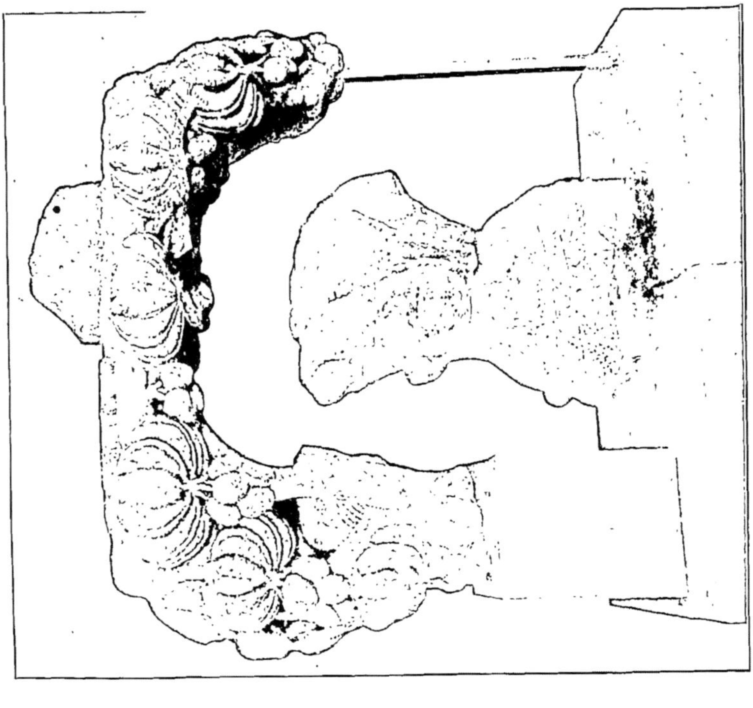

A 25 A 26

A 48.

Photo-engraved & printed at the Offices of the Survey of India, Calcutta, 192[illegible]

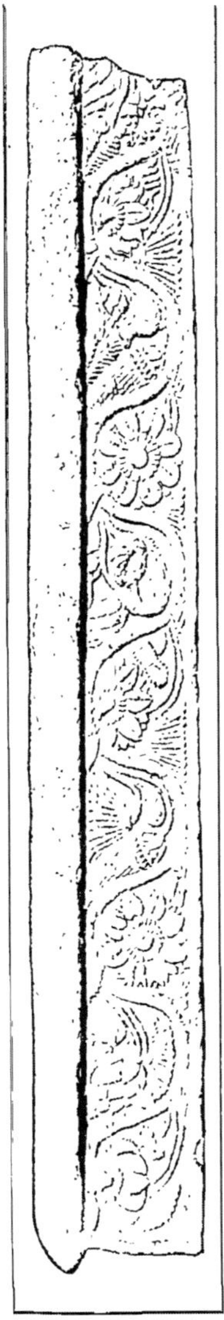

A 69

100

A 96

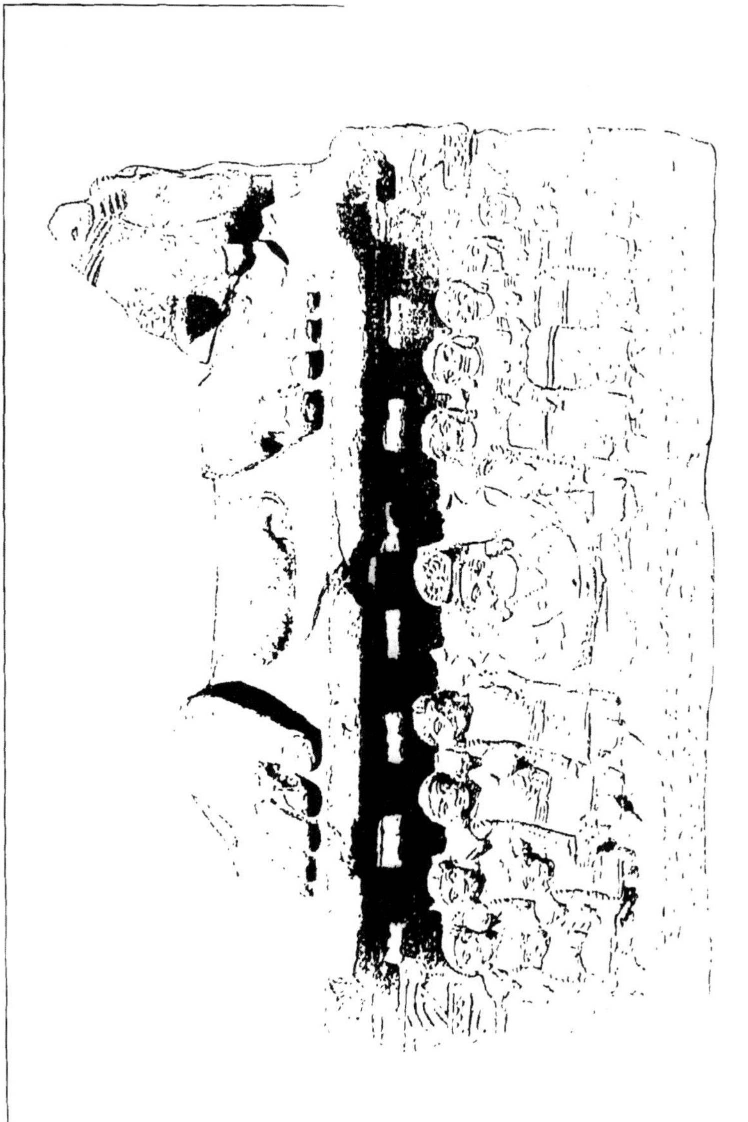

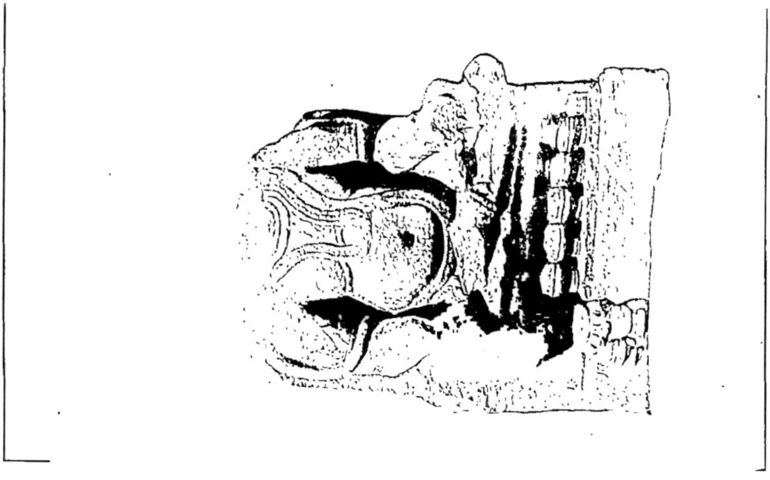

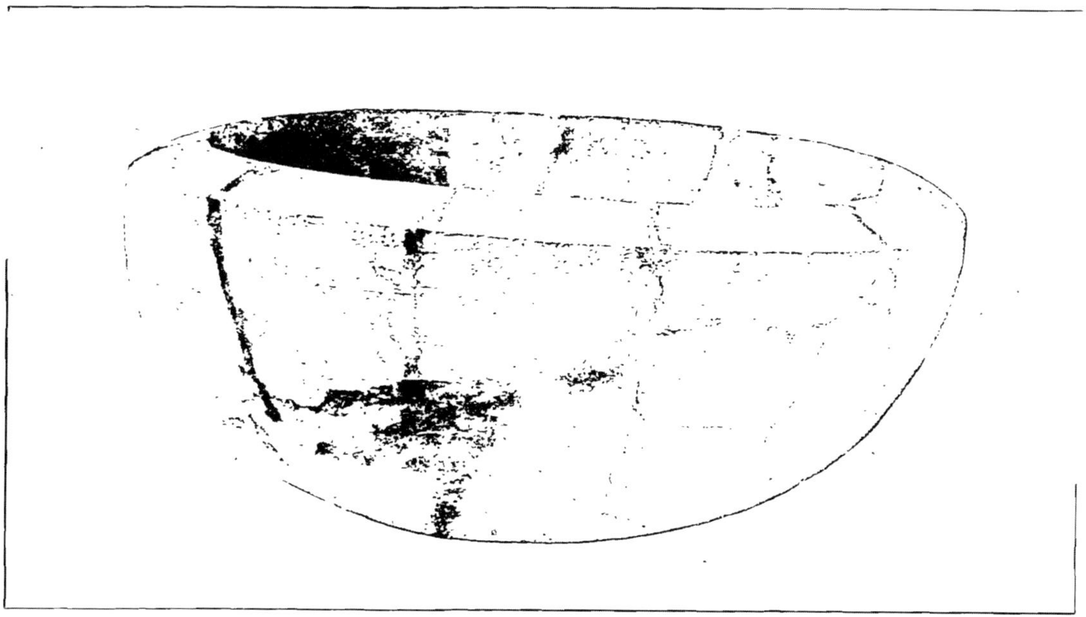

B. 1.

B 30.

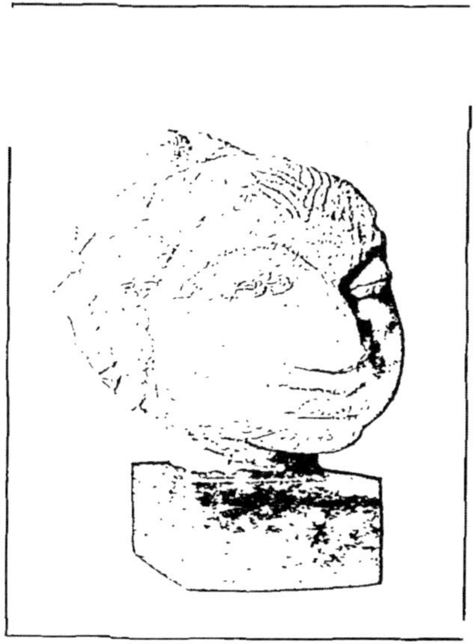

B 22

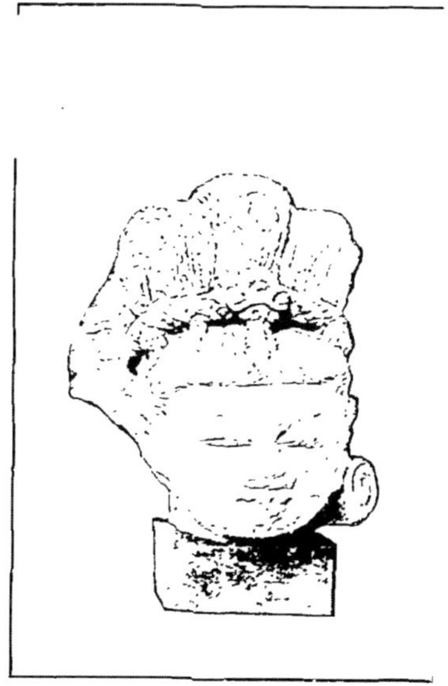

B 43.

Photo-engraved & printed at the Offices of the Survey of India, Calcutta, 1921

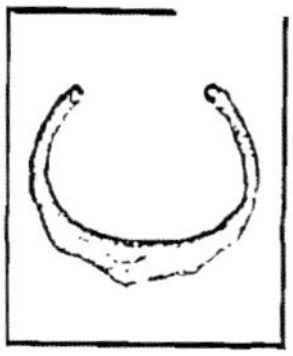

c 465

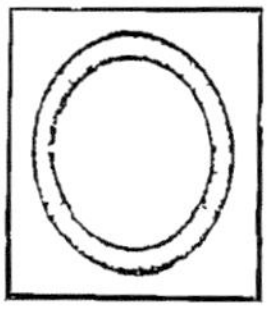

c 466

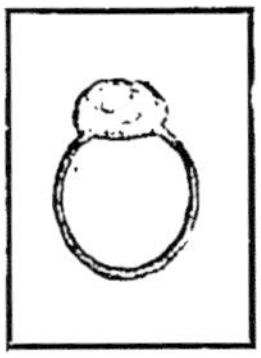

c 487

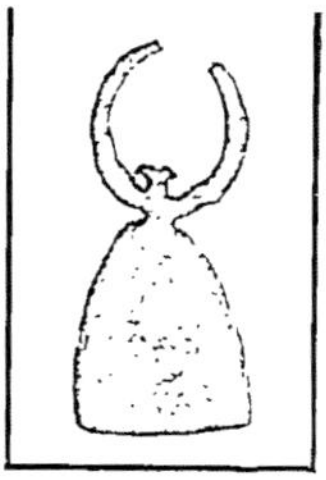

c 483

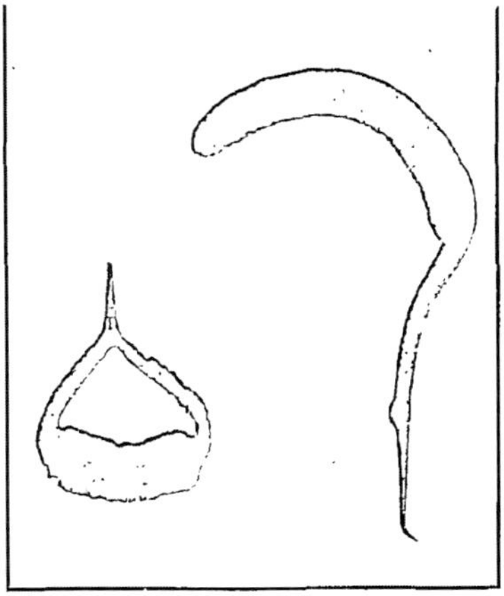

c 60 c 95

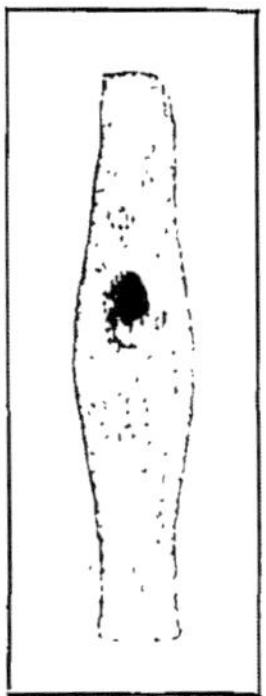

c 102

c 488

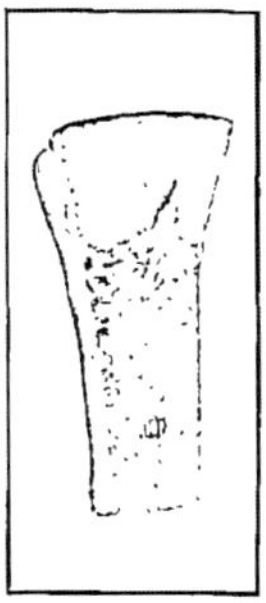

c 101

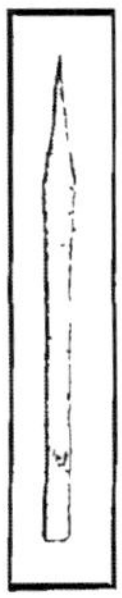

c 115

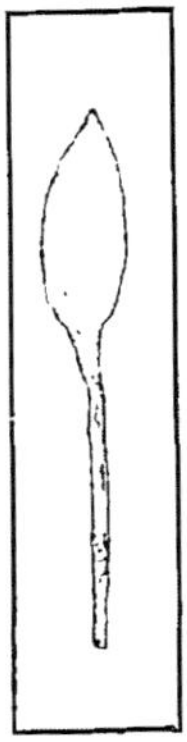

c 123

c 7

c 124

c 33

c 31

c 35

c 22

c 55

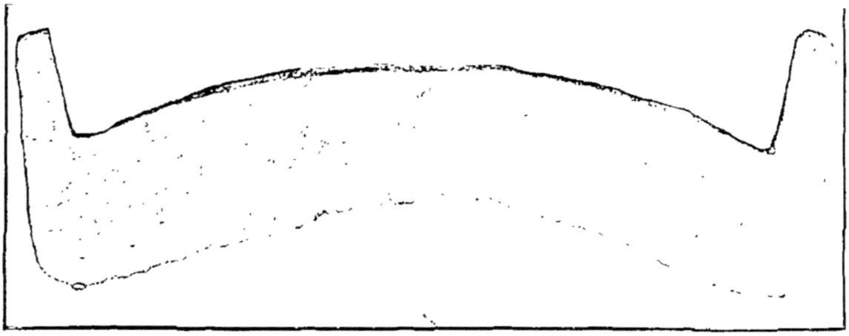

c 72

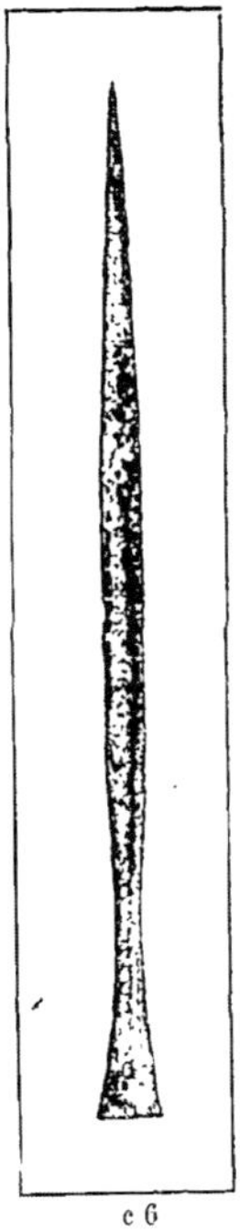

c 6

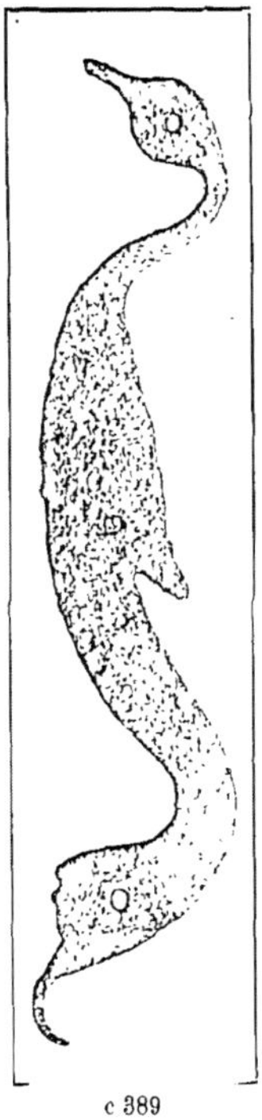

c 389

c 489

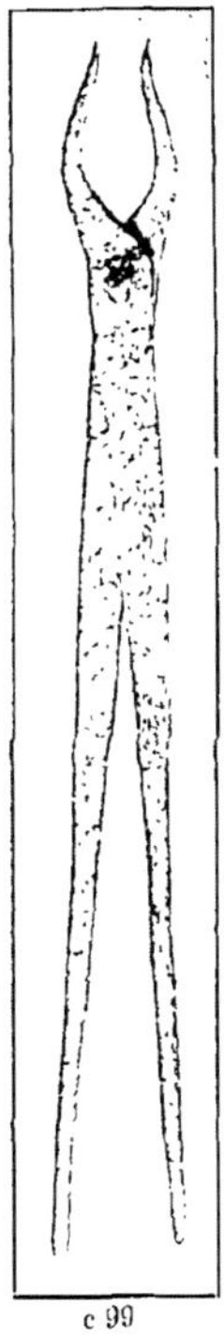

c 99

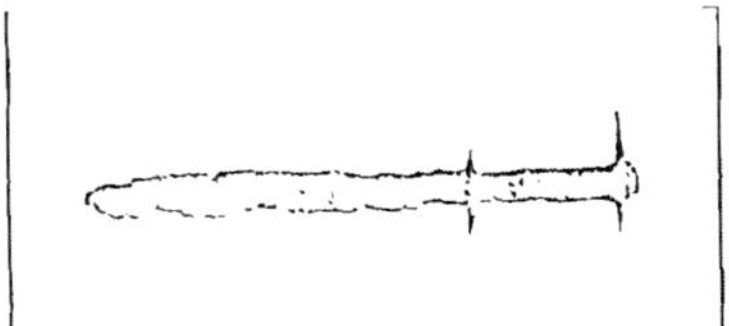

c 14

c 13

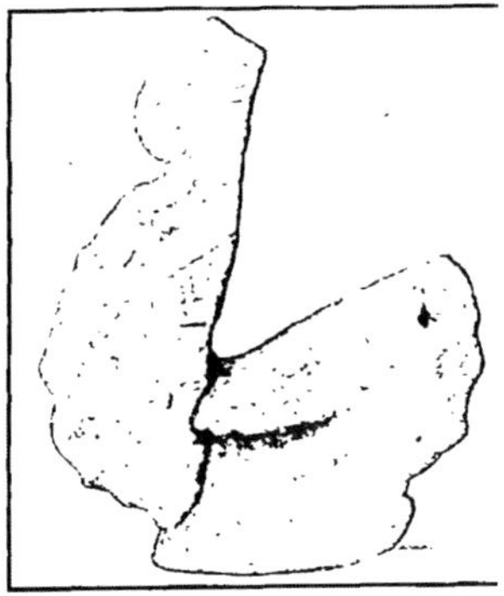

c 768-69

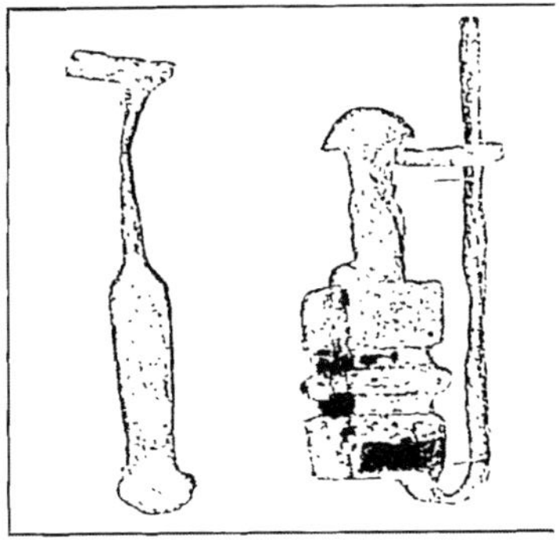

c 130 c 127

c 477

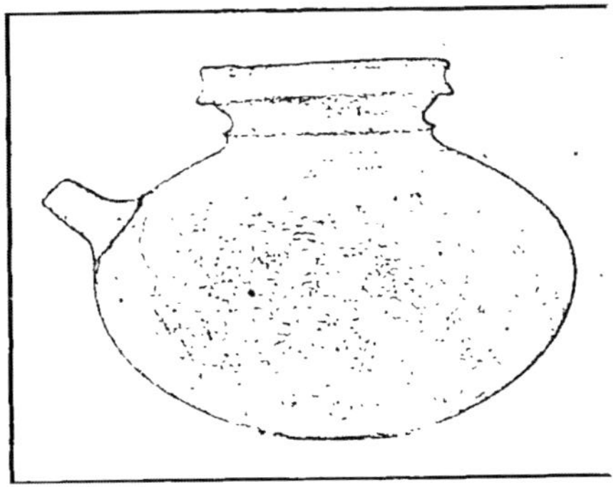

c 572

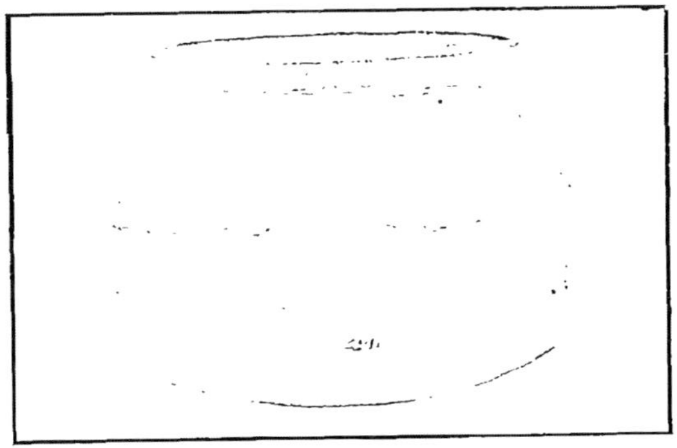

c 481

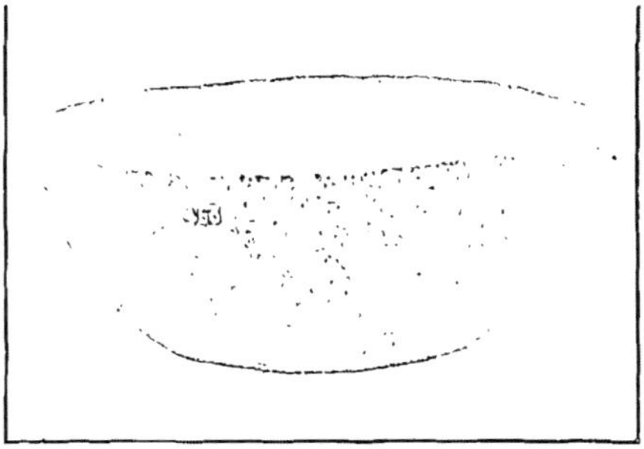

c 463

c 568

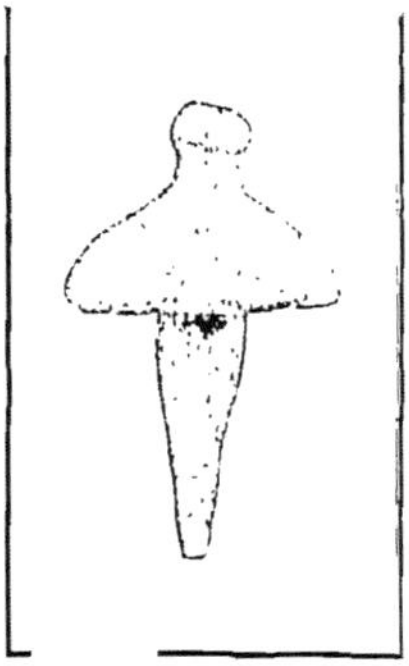

c 581

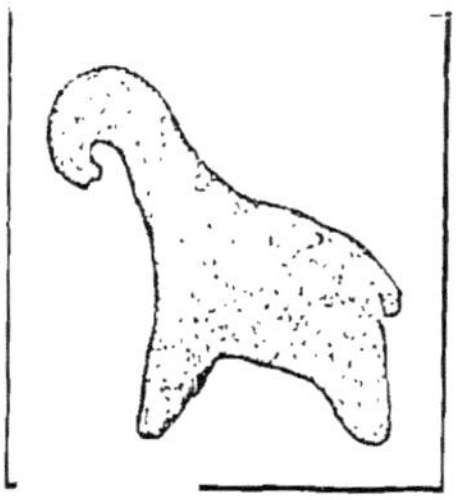

c 751

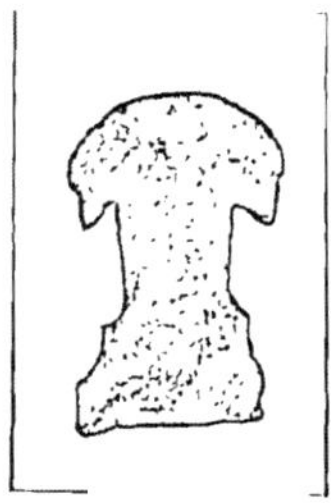

c 744

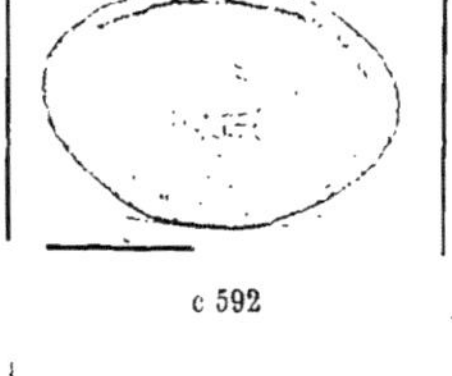

c 592

c 708

c 705

c 706

B 57

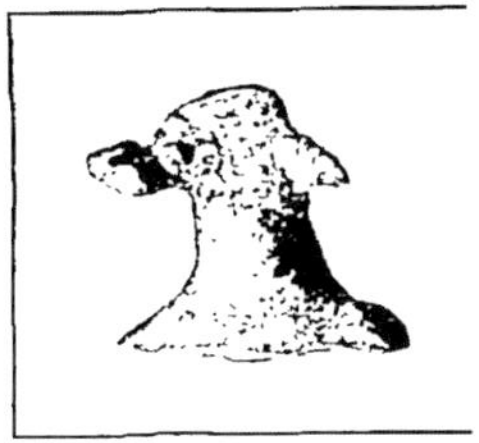

c 599.

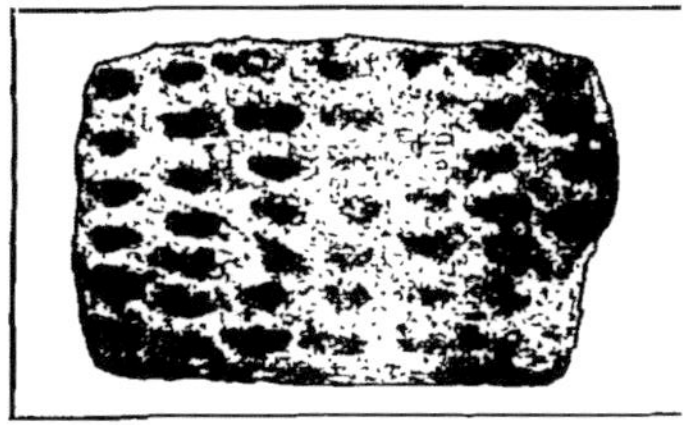

c 644.

c 540.

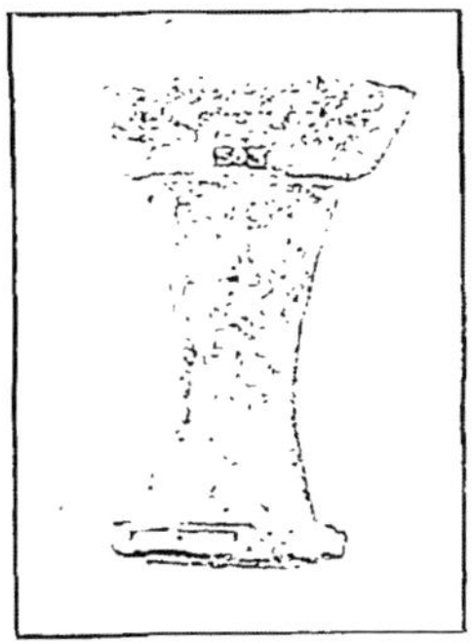

c 503.

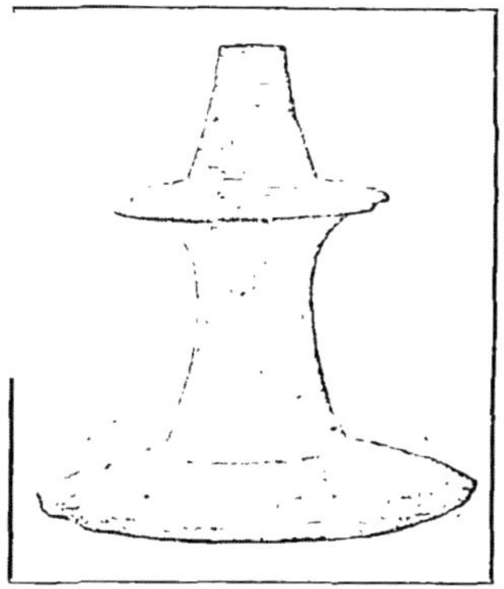

c 509.

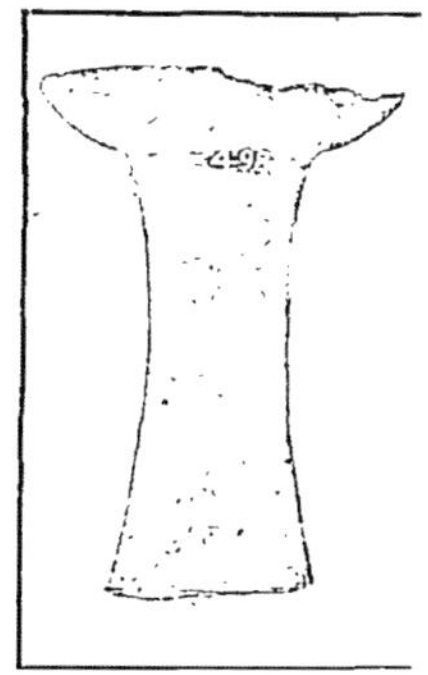

c 498.